QUESTIONS AND ANSWERS ON COLLEGE STUDENT SUICIDE:

A Law and Policy Perspective

D1414163

By Gary Pavela

The Higher Education Administration Series
Edited by Donald D. Gehring and D. Parker Young

COLLEGE ADMINISTRATION PUBLICATIONS, INC.

College Administration Publications, Inc.,
P. O. Box 9767, Asheville, N. C. 28815
Web: http://www.collegepubs.com
Email: cap@collegepubs.com

© 2006 College Administration Publications, Inc.,
All rights reserved. Published 2006
Printed in the United States of America

ISBN 0-912557-30-3

Brief quotation may be used in critical articles or reviews. For any other
reproduction of the book, including electronic, mechanical, photocopying,
recording or other means, written permission must be obtained from the
publisher.

The views expressed in this book are those of the author and are not necessarily those of College Administration Publications, Inc.

This publication is designed to provide accurate and authoritative information in regard to the subject matter covered. It is sold with the understanding that the publisher and author are not engaged in rendering legal,
accounting or other professional service. If legal advice or other expert assistance is required, the services of a competent professional person should
be sought.

*—from a Declaration of Principles jointly adopted by a committee of the
American Bar Association and a committee of publishers.*

For Margaret and the three boys

"I long ago abandoned the notion of a life without storms, or a world without dry and killing seasons. Life is too complicated, too constantly changing to be anything but what it is ... There will always be propelling, disturbing elements, and they will be there until, as Lowell puts it, the watch is taken from the wrist. It is, at the end of the day, the individual moments of restlessness, of bleakness, and of strange persuasions and maddened enthusiams, that inform one's life, change the nature and direction of one's work, and give final meaning and color to one's loves and friendships."

Kay Redfield Jamison, *An Unquiet Mind*

Table of Contents

Questions and Answers on College Student Suicide . . .

Preface

This monograph is designed to be a resource to practitioners in three professions: College administrators, attorneys, and mental health professionals. Administrators wanting a broad overview of the topic may prefer to read the questions and answers, making only occasional reference to the notes (many contain added commentary on matters of special interest, such as manic depressive illness and artistic temperament). It was anticipated, however, that lawyers and mental health professionals would value full citations and additional references to pertinent cases and professional literature.

Gary Pavela

About the Author

GARY PAVELA has been an administrator and teacher at the University of Maryland for over 25 years. He holds a M.A. in intellectual history from Wesleyan University, a law degree from the University of Illinois, and has been a Fellow at the University of Wisconsin Center for Behavioral Science and Law. He is a former law clerk to Judge Alfred P. Murrah of the United States Court of Appeals for the Tenth Circuit and has been a faculty member for the Federal Judicial Center in Washington, D.C.

In 2002 Gary Pavela was designated a Fellow of the National Association of College and University Attorneys. Fellows of the Association are identified as individuals who have "brought distinction to higher education and to the practice of law on behalf of colleges and universities across the nation." In 2005 he was awarded NASPA's "Outstanding Contribution to Literature and Research Award." He currently serves on the Board of the Kenan Institute for Ethics at Duke University.

Chapter I

Questions and Answers
on College Student Suicide:
A Law and Policy Perspective

1. HOW COMMON IS SUICIDE
AMONG TEENAGERS AND YOUNG ADULTS?

Public attention to a crisis sometimes intensifies after the crisis has peaked. In the case of completed suicides among teenagers and young adults, national data show a modest decline in suicide rates beginning in the early 1990s.[1] The current downward trend, however, comes after a tripling of the youth suicide rate between 1950 and 1994.[2] Youth suicide constitutes what the Centers for Disease Control and Prevention (CDC) calls "a major public health problem" in the United States[3]—and remains the third leading cause of death in the 15-24 age group, after unintentional injuries and homicide.[4]

News accounts of individual incidents sometimes create the impression that college students are more likely to commit suicide than their non-college attending peers. Researchers agree, however, that college students commit suicide at about half the rate of young adults who are not attending college.[5] Reasons for the difference may include limited access to firearms in collegiate settings; stronger family support networks among college-attending youth; greater involvement by pre-college and college students in clubs and sports;[6] greater access to antidepressant medications; and the increased availability of peer, academic, and professional counseling.

Data about completed suicides should not be confused with rates of depression and contemplated suicide among college students. Some observers see a significant increase in rates of depression (nearly 1 in 2 students becoming "severely depressed" during their undergraduate years) with about 10 percent of college students reporting that they had "seriously considered" suicide.[7] Other reports indicate that "college freshmen's self-reported emotional well-being hit a 'record low'"

1

in recent years, and that visits to college counseling centers have increased dramatically since 1995.[8]

What policy conclusions can be drawn from the data? First, youth suicide is a serious national health problem. The problem is not new. It has deep social roots, extending back several decades, grounded, perhaps, in changes in American family structures.[9] From a statistical perspective, colleges and universities are not incubators of youth suicide. If anything, the collegiate environment may reduce suicide risk. Complacency, however, is not appropriate, both in light of the tragedy each suicide represents, and warning signs about higher rates of depression and stress among contemporary college students.

2. CAN SUICIDE BE PREDICTED?

In a word: No. College administrators should not assume that mental health professionals (or anyone else) can make credible long-term predictions about a student's future behavior. Studies have shown that even among populations at high risk for suicide, completed suicides are too rare to support any reliable predictive models.[10] A definitive statement on suicide prediction and prevention was issued by the American Psychiatric Association (APA) in 2003 ("Practice Guideline for the Assessment and Treatment of Patients With Suicidal Behaviors")[11]. A review of the APA Practice Guideline (Guideline) in the July 2004 issue of *Psychiatric Times* reported that:

> Suicidal ideation occurs in about 5.6% of the U.S. population, with about 0.7% of the population attempting suicide. The incidence of completed suicide is far lower, at 0.01%. "This rarity of suicide, even in groups known to be at higher risk than the general population, contributes to the impossibility of predicting suicide," according to the [G]uideline.[12]

One factor limiting the effectiveness of suicide prediction is the impulsive nature of most suicides. Psychiatry Professor (and 2001 MacArthur Fellow) Kay Redfield Jamison at the Johns Hopkins University School of Medicine has written that:

> [W]e know that suicidal acts are often impulsive; that is they are undertaken without much forethought or regard for consequence. More than half of suicide attempts occur in a context of a premeditation period of less than five minutes.[13]

While students with certain mood disorders (or with unusually sensitive or volatile personalities) may have a lower threshold for suicide, they may also react to stress by engaging in spontaneous acts of creativity (writing a poem and seeking religious inspiration). Indeed, one of the chief aims of therapy is to help patients channel their emotions in precisely that way. Mood disorders are so widespread[14]; stress so ubiquitous; impulsiveness so common (especially among adolescents); and suicide so comparatively infrequent that predicting which person at greater statistical risk for suicide will actually commit suicide is impossible, at least with current predictive models.

The inability to predict suicide has not prevented mental health professionals from trying to identify *risk factors* for suicide. Four risk factors cited by The Jed Foundation ("a nonprofit public charity committed to reducing the youth suicide rate") are:

- Mental Illness: 90% of adolescent suicide victims have at least one diagnosable, active psychiatric illness at the time of death—most often depression, substance abuse, and conduct disorders. Only 15% of suicide victims were in treatment at the time of death.

- Previous Attempts: 26-33% of adolescent suicide victims have made a previous suicide attempt.

- Stressors: Suicide in youth often occurs after the victim has gotten into some sort of trouble or has experienced a recent disappointment or rejection.

- Firearms: Having a firearm in the home greatly increases the risk of youth suicide. 64% of suicide victims 10-24 years old use a firearm to complete the act."[15]

Other frequently cited risk factors include:

- A family history of suicide;[16]

- Recent suicide of a close friend or relation;

- Social stresses associated with being gay or bisexual;

- Legal problems or disciplinary incidents;

- Physical or sexual abuse in childhood;

- Persistent anxiety or panic attacks;

- Demonstrated high levels of aggression and impulsiveness;[17]

- Health problems or disabilities, especially if associated with shame or humiliation.

Individual risk factors can be exacerbated by general environmental conditions, especially seasonality (peak months for suicide are late spring and summer)[18] and dramatic or romanticized publicity about recent suicides.[19]

Identifying "risk factors" for suicide can expedite a decision to refer a student for further assessment. The aim of undertaking more detailed suicide risk assessment is to gather sufficient information to implement appropriate interventions and treatment plans. The APA document "Assessing and Treating Suicidal Behaviors: A Quick Reference Guide" (based on the Guideline) contains a series of questions mental health professionals may ask persons referred for assessment. The questions include:

- Have you ever felt that life was not worth living?
- Did you ever wish you could go to sleep and just not wake up?
- Is death something you've thought about recently?
- Have things ever reached the point that you've thought of harming yourself?

[For individuals who have thoughts of self-harm or suicide, ask]:
- How often have those thoughts occurred . . .?
- How likely do you think it is that you will act on them in the future?
- Have you made a specific plan to harm or kill yourself? (If so, what does the plan include?)

The APA "Quick Reference Guide" also cautions that:

> [S]uicide assessment scales have very low predictive values and do not provide reliable estimates of suicide risk. Nonetheless, they may be useful in developing a thorough line of questioning about suicide or in opening communication with the patient."[20]

Suicide risk assessment protocols used by mental health professionals are not designed to serve the administrative purpose of screening out students at risk of suicide. Guidelines and questions that might be helpful in "opening communication" with students and establishing baseline therapeutic responses (subject to review and modification during the course of counseling and treatment) do not have sufficient predictive value to dismiss students deemed to be "at risk" of suicide[21]. Administrative decisions of that nature are better grounded on demonstrable, usually disruptive behavior (e.g. overt suicide threats or attempts), not "predictions" or "risk assessments" about what a student might do in the future.

3. IS THERE A LEGAL DUTY TO PREVENT SUICIDE?

Liability risks for suicide remain low, at least outside custodial settings where a "special relationship" is likely to arise (e.g. hospitals or inpatient facilities)[22] or when the suicide is "caused" by a defendant (for example, by "illegal and careless" dissemination of drugs)[23] or when a mental health professional fails to meet established standards of diagnosis or care.[24] Current law in the higher education setting was summarized by the Supreme Court of Iowa in *Jain v. State of Iowa* (2000), when it held that knowledge by university officials of a prior suicide attempt in the residence halls by an 18-year-old freshman (Sanjay Jain) did not create a "special relationship" giving rise to a duty of care.

The *Jain* court observed that "[i]n Iowa and elsewhere, it is the general rule that . . . the act of suicide is considered a deliberate, intentional and intervening act that precludes another's responsibility for the harm."[25] The court applied this principle even though university staff members failed to notify Sanjay's parents about his prior suicide attempt, as institutional policies apparently required.

The record, read in the light most favorable to the plaintiff, reveals that Sanjay may have been at risk of harming himself. No affirmative action by the defendant's employees, however, *increased* that risk of self-harm. To the contrary, it is undisputed that the RAs appropriately intervened in an emotionally-charged situation, offered Sanjay support and encouragement, and referred him to counseling. Beth Merritt [the hall residence coordinator] likewise counseled Sanjay to talk things over with his parents, seek professional help, and call her at any time ...

She sought Sanjay's permission to contact his parents but he refused. In short, no action by university personnel prevented Sanjay from taking advantage of the help and encouragement being offered, nor did they do anything to prevent him from seeking help on his own accord. The record is similarly devoid of any proof that Sanjay relied, to his detriment, on the services gratuitously offered by these same personnel. To the contrary, it appears by all accounts that he failed to follow up on recommended counseling or seek the guidance of his parents, as he assured the staff he would do ... (emphasis supplied). [26]

The court in *Jain* faced emotionally compelling factual circumstances in which "plaintiff's contention[s] carrie[d] considerable appeal."[27] Nonetheless, it remained unwilling to create a precedent that might diminish the responsibilities of college students as adults; pose substantial liability risks to schools and colleges; and promote intrusive, hair trigger responses to ambiguous behaviors that may or may not have been suicide attempts.

Suicide liability litigation against colleges continues to grow,[28] even as legal theories supporting a duty of care remain tenuous. One recent federal district court case (subsequently settled) highlights what may be an avenue for an expanded duty of care: Specific knowledge of a recent suicide attempt (suggesting "an imminent probability" of suicide), coupled with an inadequate emergency response that may have discouraged the student (or the student's friends and family) from seeking appropriate professional help. *Schieszler v. Ferrum College*[29]. The court in *Schieszler* wrote that:

While it is unlikely that Virginia would conclude that a special relationship exists as a matter of law between colleges and universities and their students, it might find that a special relationship exists on the particular facts alleged in this case. Frentzel was a full-time student at Ferrum College. He lived in an on-campus dormitory. The defendants were aware that Frentzel had emotional problems; they had required him to seek anger management counseling before permitting him to return to school for a second semester. The defendants knew that, within days of his death, Frentzel was found by campus police alone in his room with bruises on his head and that he claimed these bruises were self-inflicted. The defendants knew that, at around the same time, Frentzel had sent a message to his girlfriend, in which he stated that he intended to kill himself. The defendants knew that Frentzel had sent other communications, to his girlfriend and to another friend, suggesting that he intended to kill himself. After Frentzel was found alone in his room with bruises on his head, the defendants required Frentzel to sign a statement that he would not hurt himself.

This last fact, more than any other, indicates that the defendants believed Frentzel was likely to harm himself. Based on these alleged facts, a trier of fact could conclude that there was "an imminent probability" that Frentzel would try to hurt himself, and that the defendants had notice of this specific harm. Thus, I find that the plaintiff has alleged sufficient facts to support her claim that a special relationship existed between Frentzel and defendants giving rise to a duty to protect Frentzel from the foreseeable danger that he would hurt himself. In reaching this conclusion, I have also considered whether defendants could reasonably have foreseen that they would be expected to take affirmative action to assist Frentzel . . . It is true that colleges are not insurers of the safety of their students . . . It is also true that Ferrum did not technically stand *in loco parentis* vis-a-vis Frentzel and his fellow students. Nonetheless, "[p]arents, students, and the general community still have a reasonable expectation, fostered in part by colleges themselves, that reasonable care will be exercised to protect resident students from foreseeable harm." *Mullins v. Pine Manor College*, 449 N.E.2d 331 (1983).

Both *Schieszler* and *Mullins (supra)* were cited in a June 27, 2005 Massachusetts Superior Court summary judgment ruling in the case of *Shin v. MIT*.[30] On the issue of a duty of care on the part of MIT administrators, the court wrote that:

Section 314A of the Restatement (2nd) of Torts expressly recognizes that there exist "special relationships" which give rise to a duty to act or protect a person where otherwise no such duty would exist . . .

[For example,] in *Mullins v. Pine Manor College,* the plaintiff was abducted from her dormitory and raped by an unidentified assailant. 389 Mass 47 (1983). The SJC [Supreme Judicial Court of Massachusetts] held that the college and the administrator owed a duty to exercise care to protect the well-being of their resident students, including seeking to protect them against the criminal acts of third parties . . . The Court noted that it found the source for imposing such a duty in "existing social values and customs . . ."

More recently, in *Schieszler v. Ferrum College,* a similar case to the instant case, a U.S. District Court in Virginia denied a motion to dismiss on the issue of whether a duty was owed to a student who committed suicide ... Following an analysis similar to the SJC in *Mullins* ... the federal court concluded that the defendants owed a duty to the decedent because of a special relationship between them ... The court found that the trier of fact could conclude that there was an "imminent probability" that the decedent would try to hurt himself, and the defendants had notice of this specific harm ...

In the instant case, [named MIT administrarors] were well aware of Elizabeth's mental problems at MIT from at least February 1999 ... The plaintiffs have provided sufficient evidence that [the administrators] could reasonably foresee that Elizabeth would hurt herself without proper supervision. Accordingly, there was a "special relationship" between the MIT Administrators ... and Elizabeth imposing a duty on [the administrators] to exercise reasonable care to protect Elizabeth from harm.

The widespread coverage given to the *Shin* case may amplify the importance of this state trial court opinion. The best that can be said about national trends in the law is that liability for student suicide—currently stated with the greatest authority in *Jain v. Iowa*—appears to be questioned by courts in Massachusetts and Virginia. Suggestions of a "trend" toward expansion of duty in college student suicide cases may prove true in the end, but seem premature at present.

A suicide liability case arising in the secondary school setting in Maryland in 1991 will also be referenced in future litigation against colleges and universities. In *Eisel v. Board of Education* (1991)[31] Maryland's Court of Appeals (the state's highest court) held that junior high school counselors had a duty to alert parents to suicidal statements attributed to the parent's child by fellow students, even when the adolescent denied ever making the statements. *Eisel* is readily distinguishable from *Jain* because the school in *Eisel* stood *"in loco parentis"* with the student. Still, the analysis in *Eisel* is pertinent, since the court was influenced, in part, by state suicide prevention initiatives designed to help educators and mental health professionals respond more effectively to youth suicide. The court wrote that:

Nicole's suicide was foreseeable because the defendants allegedly had direct evidence of Nicole's intent to commit suicide. That notice to the defendants distinguishes this case from *Bogust v. Iverson* [10 Wis.2d 129, 102 N.W.2d 228 (1960)] where the [college] counselor had no notice of contemplated suicide ...

The [Maryland] General Assembly has made it quite clear that prevention of youth suicide is an important public policy, and that local schools should be at the forefront of the prevention effort ... Nicole's school had a suicide prevention program prior to her death ... [A] memorandum dated February 18, 1987, from the office of the principal to the staff of [the middle school] [addressed] the subject of "Suicide Prevention." It consists of a top sheet setting forth the "steps [that] must be followed." The top sheet is supplemented by materials on other pages reproduced from various sources. These materials include lists of the methods of, and motives for, suicide and important warning signs ("[A]lmost all who have committed suicide have communicated their intent beforehand."). Part IX lists ten answers to the question, "How Can You Help In A Suicidal Crisis?" "Answer D is: 'Tell others—As quickly as possible, share your knowledge with parents, friends, teachers or other people who might be able to help. Don't worry about breaking a confidence if someone reveals suicidal plans to you. You may have to betray a secret to save a life . . .'"

There is no indication in the Act that the Legislature intended to create a statutorily based cause of action against school counselors who negligently fail to intervene in a potential suicide. Nevertheless, holding counselors to a common law duty of reasonable care to prevent suicides when they have evidence of a suicidal intent comports with the policy underlying this Act . . .[32]

Colleges across the country are intensifying suicide prevention efforts and creating protocols requiring that students who threaten or attempt suicide be referred for prompt professional assessment. At the same time, legislation signed by President Bush on October 21, 2004 provides grants "to help states . . . and higher learning institutions fund suicide prevention and intervention programs for youth . . . The legislation has been named 'Garrett Lee Smith Memorial Act' in memory of [Senator Gordon Smith's] 21-year-old son, who took his own life last year."[33] These developments, standing alone, are unlikely to make *Eisel* a compelling precedent in the higher education setting (or elsewhere)[34]. Still, additional legislation requiring enhanced suicide prevention and parental notification procedures could create a factual analogue similar to that in *Eisel*. If so, courts—which still exhibit considerable reluctance to increase third part liability risks for suicide—may be more willing to find a "duty of care" when college officials have "direct evidence" of a student's suicidal intent.

As suggested earlier, the issue of liability for student suicide in the college and university setting is conjectural at best. While established legal precedent clearly limits the risk, early signs of change are on the horizon, intensified by growing activism among parents on the issue of campus safety and security. There is no indication courts or legislatures will impose a requirement that colleges randomly screen and predict which students will commit suicide and make timely interventions to save their lives. No other institution in society can accomplish that task, and colleges won't be seen as an exception. Nor will lay administrators or counselors be expected to know and respond to all of the evolving (and frequently ambiguous) "warning signs" of suicide.[35] Instead, institutions of higher education face heightened risk of liability for suicide when they ignore or mishandle *known suicide threats or attempts*. The immediate practical lesson for campus ad-

8   *Questions and Answers on College Student Suicide:*

ministrators (especially those supervising "gatekeepers" like resident advisors)[36] is to refrain from treating suicide threats or attempts as temporary episodes of depression or disorientation, likely to "go away" on their own[37]. What the courts may hold is what many college administrators already see: The main obstacle to better suicide prevention on campus is *underreaction*, especially the failure to provide (perhaps even require) prompt professional evaluation and treatment for any student who threatens or attempts suicide.

4. WHAT ARE THE PERTINENT LEGAL RISKS FOR COLLEGE MENTAL HEALTH PROFESSIONALS?

Mental health professionals treating outpatients now face as much risk of malpractice litigation as their colleagues treating inpatients[38]. College mental health professionals are certainly not immune, reflected in a 2005 summary judgment ruling in *Shin v. MIT*[39]. Factors exacerbating liability risks are inadequate suicide screening, failure to document suicide assessment and treatment plans, misplaced reliance upon "no harm" contracts, abandonment of students at risk of suicide, fragmented care, and lack of individualized attention and personal contact.

The general standard of care for outpatient treatment by mental health professionals was stated in a 1998 California appellate court case: *Kockelman v. Segal*[40]. The court held that:

[W]e do not by any means purport to endorse a rule which imposes an absolute duty on a psychiatrist to prevent a patient's suicide. We find only that a psychiatrist's duty of care to a patient, which may include taking appropriate suicide prevention measures if warranted by all of the circumstances, is not negated by the patient's status as an outpatient . . .[41]

The court in *Kockelman* cited *Jacoves v. United Merchandising Corp*[42]: "If those who are caring for and treating mentally disturbed patients know of facts from which they could reasonably conclude that the patient would be likely to self-inflict harm in the absence of preventative measures, then those caretakers must use reasonable care under the circumstances to prevent such harm from occurring."[43]

A primary obligation of mental health professionals providing care for students at risk of suicide is systematic, fully documented risk assessment by an experienced mental health professional[44]. The critical role of proper risk assessment was highlighted by Kay Redfield Jamison when she reported that "nearly a third of those who kill themselves visit a physician in the week before they die, and more than half do so in the month prior to committing suicide."[45]

Robert I. Simon, M.D. author of *Assessing and Managing Suicide Risk : Guidelines for Clinically Based Risk Management* (2004)[46] has written that assessment of "no risk" based "solely on the patient's denial of suicidal ideation, intent, or plan . . . is insufficient"[47]. What is required, based on a consensus of mental health professionals,[48] is an ongoing process of gathering pertinent evidence, based on the best available assessment protocols. A 2004 article in *Psychiatric Annals*[49] (reviewing the *American Psychiatric Association Practice Guideline for the Assessment and Treatment of Patients with Suicidal Behaviors*) (*Guideline*) contains the following overview:

> Areas to be evaluated during the assessment include the patient's current and past psychiatric diagnoses, with attention to any co-morbidity. Family and personal history of suicide, attempts, and mental illness, as well as individual strengths and vulnerabilities, should also be evaluated, as should acute and chronic life stressors, possible protective factors, and current complaints, symptoms, and mental state. In particular, the presence or absence of any hopelessness, anxiety, and substance use should be assessed. It is useful to evaluate suicidal thoughts, plans, and behaviors through direct questions about current and past suicidal thoughts and actions. If the patient is not forthcoming it may be necessary to seek history from collateral sources. A complete psychiatric history and evaluation is crucial to the assessment process because "the presence of a psychiatric disorder is probably the most significant risk factor for suicide . . ." [quoting the *Guideline*].[50]

Additional factors that should be considered in making a risk assessment are the quality of the working relationship between the mental health professional and the student (the "therapeutic alliance"), and special characteristics of the campus environment, including the powerful "protective factor" of restrictions on access to weapons.

Thorough assessment is of limited value without careful documentation, especially in environments where students may be in contact with several mental health professionals. Robert Simon has written in this regard that:

> If a malpractice claim is brought against the psychiatrist, contemporaneous documentation of suicide risk assessments assists the court the evaluating the many clinical complexities and ambiguities that exist in treatment and management of patients at risk of suicide. Some courts may conclude that what was not recorded has not been done. . . A psychiatrist's best friend in court is a carefully documented record that contemporaneously details the provision of reasonable care.[51]

Contemporaneous documentation must be readily available (in legible form) to other authorized members of the treatment team, and should encompass a variation of the basic formula (familiar to journalists) of "Who, What, When, Where, and Why?" The "Who" for mental health professionals should include persons who contribute to or can ameliorate the risk of suicide; the "What" should include identified risk factors, overall risk assessment, and interventions selected; the "Why" should specify the rationale for the intervention and reasons for rejecting likely alternatives[52].

The use of suicide prevention contracts is questioned in the professional literature and may enhance liability risks. Jeffrey Stovall and Frank Domino at the University of Massachusetts Medical Center recently wrote in this regard that "[t]he suicide prevention contract, although frequently used, is of unproven clinical and legal usefulness during times of increased suicide risk and generally should be avoided."[53] A particular danger in relying upon suicide prevention contracts is that they may serve as an illusory substitute for comprehensive, individualized treatment. College administrators in nontherapeutic settings may find continued value in disciplinary *behavioral* contracts, but asking students to sign "no harm" or suicide prevention contracts in lieu of professional evaluation and treatment is an invitation to institutional liability.[54]

One of the unexpected legal risks faced by college mental health professionals is a claim that they "abandoned" a student at risk of suicide. The issue has to be understood in light of data showing that most individuals who commit suicide see a mental health professional shortly before they kill themselves.[55] Students at high risk of suicide who appear at a counseling center or mental health clinic need prompt, professional evaluation and treatment. If those services aren't available on campus, some plan must be in place to provide them without delay at the closest feasible location.

Many colleges have policies limiting the amount of counseling and therapy available. There's nothing inherently unreasonable with that approach, provided ample notice is provided to current and prospective students.[56] What would be inadvisable, however, is to follow a rigid policy of enforcing a pre-determined number of health or counseling center visits by a student at risk of suicide. Robert I. Simon has stated what is likely to be the standard of care in this regard:

> If the therapist simply abandons the patient after insurance coverage ends, the liability risk is high ... The therapist's duty of care to the patient is not defined or limited by managed care [MCO] arrangements. Clinics or group practices should not have policies that call for the summary discharge of patients when insurance benefits end. Such policies are invitations for lawsuits alleging negligent treatment and abandonment ...[57]

Simon is not contending that students at risk of suicide can never be referred elsewhere. He does conclude, however, that "the referral option may not be feasible until the patient's current suicide crisis has passed."[58]

Continuity of care as well as building and maintaining a therapeutic alliance between student and mental health professional is important. Any change in setting and service should be done after individualized assessment, with the margin of error tipping in favor of providing ongoing support to a student at risk of suicide.

Students who might eventually be referred to other health care providers must be referred with care. An example of potential problems that may arise can be found in a 1998 Rhode Island Supreme Court decision *Klein v. Solomon*[59]. In *Klein*, a "very accomplished" student (Daniel Schuster) with "psychological problems [from] an early age" chose to enroll at Brown University "partly because of the psychological and psychiatric services it offered." Daniel was seen at Brown by a psychologist and professor of psychology (Ferdinand Jones), who learned of Daniel's extensive psychological history, including feelings of "anxiety and dread," depression, and recurring "suicidal fantasies." In the words of the court:

> Despite these obvious warning signals that should have alerted Jones to Daniel's predilection for suicide, Jones saw Daniel just three times, in keeping with Brown's policy that its psychological services be available only for short-term care. At the third meeting Jones gave Daniel a list of four people that he could contact for further treatment. None of those four people were psychiatrists, and in fact only three were psychologists. None specialized in suicide prevention. Daniel chose Mark Solomon (Solomon), whose specialty was in eating disorders . . . Solomon treated Daniel for over two years. Daniel then terminated his treatment with Solomon and two weeks later committed suicide.[60]

On the issue of liability for "negligent referral" (resolved in favor of Brown by a lower court) the Rhode Island Supreme Court wrote that:

> We conclude that the trial justice erred in this case and that legally sufficient evidence existed in the record on the issue of Jones's alleged negligent referral. Jones wrote in his notes from his scheduled appointments with Daniel that Daniel had suicidal fantasies and that he was depressed and anxious. That evidence would be enough to put Jones on notice of Daniel's potential for suicide. A jury certainly could have reasonably concluded that Jones was negligent in failing to refer Daniel to someone qualified in suicide prevention or to someone who could prescribe medication for Daniel that would reduce his suicidal inclinations.[61]

In many instances, students at high risk of suicide should be hospitalized rather than referred for outpatient treatment. The decision to suggest or require hospitalization entails professional judgment and cannot be definitively codified.[62] Hospitalization should not be undertaken primarily as a risk management strategy;[63] neither should it be rejected due to fear of embarrassment, inconvenience, or "One Flew

Questions and Answers on College Student Suicide:

Over the Cuckoo's Nest" stereotypes. A powerful insight in this regard can be found in William Styron's book *Darkness Visible* (a story of his battle with clinical depression). Reflecting upon his depression, his preparations to commit suicide, and the timely intervention of his wife (who arranged admission to a hospital) Styron wrote that:

> Many psychiatrists, who simply do not seem to be able to comprehend the nature and depth of the anguish their patients are undergoing, maintain their stubborn allegiance to pharmaceuticals in the belief that eventually the pills will kick in, the patient will respond, and the somber surroundings of the hospital will be avoided . . . [I]n fact, the hospital was my salvation, and it is something of a paradox that in this austere place with its locked and wired doors and desolate green hallways—ambulances screeching night and day ten floors below—I found the repose, the assuagement of the tempest in my brain, that I was unable to find in my [home] . . . [T]he hospital . . . offers the mild, oddly gratifying trauma of sudden stabilization . . . into an orderly and benign detention where one's only duty is to get well.[64]

Finally, the dangers of fragmented care rival those of abandonment, and may present comparable liability risks. Indeed, the question of "fragmented care" appears to be at the core of alleged medical malpractice in the widely publicized case of *Shin v. MIT*[65]. Generally, the most effective therapeutic responses to depression entail some combination of medication and talk therapy.[66] Both approaches depend in varying degrees upon an effective therapeutic alliance between individual students and their therapists. That alliance will rarely be created or maintained if students seeking ongoing therapy encounter multiple harried practitioners reading hasty notes left by distracted colleagues. The result is not only inferior treatment, but greater risk of litigation when treatment is questioned.[67] This perspective was summarized by Robert I. Simon in a May 2004 article in *Psychiatric Times*:

> While it important to know the patient's disease, it is essential to know the patient with the disease. The psychiatrist must be able to commit the necessary time and effort to properly treat the patient at risk for suicide. Good clinical care is always the best risk management.[68]

5. SHOULD COLLEGES NOTIFY PARENTS OF STUDENTS AT RISK OF SUICIDE?

For growing numbers of college administrators the answer is *yes*, unless the information is privileged as a matter of law.[69] The topic is more of a policy question than a legal issue, since the Family Educational Rights and Privacy Act (FERPA) permits (but does not require) parental notification if parents claim the student as a dependent for tax purposes,[70] or in emergencies.[71] Each campus should address this issue in an annual notification statement to students.[72]

Attitudes toward parental notification vary over time and are undergoing a national seismic shift.[73] The notion that full adulthood is bestowed as an act of nature at the stroke of midnight on the eighteenth birthday is passing quickly from the cultural scene. An article in the January 2, 2002 *Washington Post*[74] reported in this regard that:

> The Society for Adolescent Medicine, a physician's organization, now says . . . that it cares for persons "10 to 26 years of age." A National Academy of Sciences Committee, surveying programs for adolescents, discussed extending its review to age 30 . . . The MacArthur Foundation has funded a $3.4 million project called "Transitions to Adulthood," which pegs the end of that transition at 34.[75]

Some observers see the expansion of adolescence as a peculiar American phenomenon, associated with evolving cultural patterns of baby boomers and their offspring. Another explanation is that American society is converging with many other parts of the world, where young adults often stay at home as part of an extended family. The January 2, 2002 *Post* article cited Spain and Poland as examples, and also reported "[i]n Italy, the average age to leave Mom and Dad is 34 years."[76]

Educators also need to know that students' attitudes toward their parents vary by generational cohort. The sense of rebellion older college administrators displayed thirty or forty years ago is far less evident among the "Millennials" (a leading edge of college students born in 1982). Neil Howe and William Strauss, authors of *Millennials Rising*[77] report in this regard that "[m]ost [Millennials] say they identify with their parents' values, and over nine in ten say they 'trust' . . . their parents."[78]

It would be simpler for college administrators if traditional age students were full adults. Those students could assert all the prerogatives of adulthood, and administrators could support them. Most educators, however, see traditional age students as being in a transitional stage between adolescence and adulthood.[79] During the period of that transition, colleges need to form partnerships with parents to help students navigate the demands of college life.[80]

Forming partnerships with parents will entail introducing them to developmental theories stressing the value of giving young adults greater autonomy, including the freedom to fail. At the same time, educators will need to listen to parental perspectives about the wisdom of surrendering and sharing authority gradually, not all-at-once, on some specified birthday. These discussions are already occurring across the country, producing a workable compromise: Parents will

Questions and Answers on College Student Suicide:

not be notified about minor lapses by their offspring, but they will be informed when serious single incidents or patterns of behavior indicate the student poses a substantial risk to self or others.

Whatever parental notification policies are adopted, special attention needs to be paid to alerting parents of international students or recent immigrants about them. Many will assume a liberal notification policy is in place unless informed otherwise.[81]

The issue of parental notification is especially important in suicide prevention, and often becomes the focus of litigation following a student suicide. The leading example is the suicide of Elizabeth Shin at MIT in 2000, described in a January 30, 2002 *Boston Globe* article by *Globe* columnist Eileen McNamara.[82] Ms. McNamara reported that the parents of Elizabeth Shin had filed suit against MIT, claiming the university should have told them that their daughter was profoundly depressed. Doing so, the parents claim, could have allowed them to intervene before Ms. Shin set herself on fire and killed herself in her residence hall room.

Ms. McNamara wrote that:

> If the 19-year-old biology major was as determined to conceal her self-destructive impulses as MIT contends, why were they so well known on the campus? If hers was so hopeless a case of depression, why wouldn't Shin's therapists have sought a last-ditch alliance with the people who knew her best, her parents? ... The aspiring geneticist did not want her parents to know how despondent she was in the weeks before she set herself on fire in her dorm room on April 10, 2000. But isn't a doctor's first obligation to a patient's survival, not her confidentiality? ... Dr. Paul R. McHugh thinks so. "Privacy isn't everything; life is everything," says the former chairman of the department of psychiatry at Johns Hopkins School of Medicine, who was named last week to the President's Council on Bioethics. "We lock people up, we take their civil liberties away if they are a danger to themselves. But we can't call the parents? What kind of nonsense is that?"[83]

Published accounts of the Shin suicide at MIT suggest that none of the therapists and administrators who were aware of her distress saw her with sufficient consistency and frequency to understand the depth of the crisis she was facing[84]. Few campuses have the resources to undertake such a task, even though doing so could make a difference between life and death for troubled students. The implications are clear: Greater parental involvement in student life is more than a generational fad. Especially in the case of student suicide, the involvement of parents reflects an *adaptive survival strategy* in a world of heightened stress and diminished community. College administrators should facilitate this strategy (absent a history of parental abuse or neglect) by providing lawful notice to parents of students at high risk of suicide.[85]

A distinction needs to be made between policies designed to facilitate parental notification by administrators and the confidentiality requirements campus mental health professionals have with students in therapeutic relationships[86]. Nonetheless, while courts have been reluctant to impose a "duty to warn" on mental health professionals in cases involving "suicidal tendencies,"[87] there may be circumstances where ethical principles permit [88] and good clinical practice requires mental health professions to notify the parents of a patient. Robert I. Simon has written in this regard that:

> Management for patients at high risk for suicide may require breaking patient confidence and involving the family or significant others (e.g. to obtain vital information, to administer and monitor medications, to remove lethal weapons, to assist in hospitalization). Statutory waiver of confidential information is provided in some states when a patient seriously threatens self-harm.[89]

Parental notification by mental health professionals without student consent will be guided by state law. Consultation with legal counsel is imperative.

6. SHOULD COLLEGES WITHDRAW STUDENTS WHO THREATEN OR ATTEMPT SUICIDE?

On rare occasions a student at risk for suicide might be required to leave campus, especially if continued enrollment (even with reasonable accommodation for a mental disability) would pose a direct threat to self or others. It would, however, be ethically indefensible, legally questionable, and educationally unsupportable to automatically withdraw students thought to be at risk of suicide. The educational enterprise involves more than screening out potential liability risks. Educators have a responsibility to help students learn how to adapt to stress—turning failures and frailties into the capacity for self-insight, human connection, creativity, and productive work. [90]

From an ethical perspective, students are ends in themselves, not instruments of institutional aims. Categorical rules in this regard, of course, have to be balanced against the institution's legitimate interest in self-preservation, and the need to protect others from violence or disruptive behavior. The crux of the balance can be found in language drawn from disability law: Important administrative decisions about students must be made with due process and careful deliberation, based on individualized assessment, including assessment of the nature and expense of any reasonable accommodation. An ethical perspective would also encompass some concept of reciprocity (how would educators reasonably expect their offspring to be treated in comparable situations?) and timeless wisdom from the medical profession: *First do no harm.*

The implementation of an inflexible, automatic dismissal policy for suicide threats and attempts would violate all of these ethical principles. Such dismissal policies, usually grounded in fear, seek speed and uniformity at the expense of disciplined examination of the facts, including review of individualized diagnoses, prior patterns of behavior, levels of peer and family support, and contextual circumstances (e.g. a possible isolated event precipitating a single impulsive statement or act). Invoking an automatic dismissal policy for suicide threats and attempts means treating students more like things than persons —a practice most people (including those who design "single-sanction" or "one strike" policies) seek to avoid in their own lives.[91] It is precisely these ethical deficiencies that set the stage for a broad array of unintended consequences, including unnecessary litigation and long term damage to individual and institutional reputations.

An example of the hazards of automatic dismissal policies can be seen in July 9, 2003 *New York Times* article about an "A" student with perfect SAT scores at Phillips Academy (Cathy Rampell) who was upset about the end of "her first true romance" and labeled a suicide threat by the school psychologist.[92] After rejecting Ms. Rampell's parents' request for a second opinion, the psychologist invoked the school's "inflexible" school policy on "students at risk for suicide," requiring Ms. Rampell "to leave campus immediately" and barring her from re-admission for 16 months. The result was a full court press from Ms. Rampell's parents—and a media firestorm for Phillips Academy. The *Times* reported that Ms. Rampell's parents arranged for her to be evaluated by four psychiatrists, "three of them Harvard Medical School professors:"

> While noting Cathy was "high strung" and had a bout with anorexia as a younger teenager, all four concluded she was not suffering depression nor at risk for suicide ... One of the psychiatrists, Dr. John Maltsberger, a national expert on suicide, wrote, "The patient never had a correct suicide risk assessment ..." adding that [the school psychologist's] "alliance with this patient broke down and the patient fell into a rage with her and refused to answer questions." He indicated surprise that Cathy was not also assessed by a psychiatrist ... Another, Dr. John Julian, wrote, "in conclusion, the patient is suffering from the loss of an adolescent first love."[93]

Notwithstanding these expert assessments, and the family's willingness to sign a liability waiver, Phillips planned to proceed with the mandatory sixteen month dismissal, "pointing out no one had ever appealed a suicide-risk determination." The Rampell family then hired a prominent lawyer to write the appeal. "Suddenly," according to the

Times, "the school was willing to budge. Within weeks, the school reversed itself and agreed to let Cathy return in September." Total cost to the Rampell family "in legal, medical and other fees" was $100,000. Meanwhile, Ms. Rampell maintained her "A" average and was eventually admitted to Princeton.[94]

The basis for possible legal action in the Phillips Academy case could have been an implied covenant of fair dealing[95]. Additionally, colleges and universities (public or private) that are quick to remove students at risk of suicide may be accountable for violating Section 504 of the Rehabilitation Act of 1973 (Section 504) and the Americans with Disabilities Act (ADA).[96] Public institutions are also vulnerable to substantive or procedural due process complaints.[97] These are credible legal risks grounded on established precedents; they must be weighed against what remains, in most states, a largely hypothetical cause of action against colleges or universities for failing to prevent suicide.

Probably the greatest legal hazard faced by institutions that routinely dismiss students at risk of suicide is a violation of Section 504, enforced by the U.S. Department of Education, Office for Civil Rights (OCR). In a June 29, 2001 enforcement letter to Woodbury University in California (involving a student with a psychological disability who was excluded from the residence halls during an intersession period after she engaged in "self-injuring behavior")[98] OCR wrote that:

> OCR has long made clear that nothing in Section 504 of the Rehabilitation Act prevents educational institutions from addressing dangers posed by an individual who represents a "direct threat" to the health and safety of others, or individuals whose dangerous conduct violates an essential code of conduct provision, even if such an individual is a person with a disability. A "direct threat" is a significant risk of causing substantial harm to the health or safety of the student or others that cannot be eliminated or reduced to an acceptable level through the provision of reasonable accommodations . . .

> With regard to allegations of self-destructive conduct by an individual with a disability, OCR will accord significant discretion to decisions of post-secondary institutions made through a due process proceeding that incorporates the following basic principles.

> An institution may make inquiry into a student's medical history and records to the extent necessary to determine the conditions and circumstances under which the student may constitute a threat to him/herself (or others), the probabilities for those conditions and circumstances occurring if the student is allowed to participate in the program under consideration, and any accommodations or mitigating measures that would enable the student to meet the institution's essential academic and technical standards for participation in that program . . .

[I]nquiry into a student's medical condition may take place because the student has put his/her disability into issue in a code of conduct hearing or other procedure to ascertain direct threat to his or her own health and safety or because the University, on a nondiscriminatory basis, believes that the student represents a direct threat to him/herself. A nondiscriminatory belief will be based on a student's observed conduct, actions, and statements, not merely knowledge that the student is an individual with a disability ...

The determination of whether an individual is qualified to remain in a program because he/she may represent a direct threat to him/herself should take into account the differences in various settings in which the student may be situated. For example, a student may constitute a threat to him/herself when is a dormitory, but not when in the classroom ...

[A]lthough there is no inherent reason that issues particular to students with disabilities cannot be heard in the pertinent traditional due process forums, both the institution and the student may be better served by referring such issues to forums staffed by college personnel with more expertise in and familiarity with such issues. However, such non-traditional forums cannot deny the student with a disability the same opportunity as any other student to challenge the truth and accuracy of the accusations concerning his/her conduct and its perceived dangerousness.[99]

Serious suicide threats or attempts are usually associated with a mental disability.[100] At a minimum, students who threaten or attempt suicide will be regarded as having such a disability, thereby prompting likely application of Section 504.[101] The basic due process guidelines established by OCR for assessing whether a student "may represent a direct threat to him/herself"under Section 504 are comparable to what might be expected in a disciplinary case involving possible suspension or expulsion.

Furthermore, "direct threat" analysis in itself is painstaking, highly individualized, and contextual, including analysis of "various settings in which the student may be situated," and the requirement to consider "reasonable accommodation."[102] In short, given the additional challenges associated with predicting future behavior[103] and the impulsive nature of many suicide threats and attempts, college administrators will find that direct threat analysis (standing alone) is a daunting task.

An example of the difficulties entailed in "direct threat" analysis can also be seen in the "EEOC Enforcement Guidance on the Americans with Disabilities Act and Psychiatric Disabilities."[104] Based on reasoning in pertinent OCR letters to colleges and universities, the analysis here (in question and answer format) will also be applicable to students in the higher education setting:

Does an individual who has attempted suicide pose a direct threat when s/he seeks to return to work?

No, in most circumstances. As with other questions of direct threat, an employer must base its determination on an individualized assessment of the person's ability to safely perform job functions when s/he returns to work. Attempting suicide does not mean that an individual poses an imminent risk of harm to him/herself when s/he returns to work. In analyzing direct threat (including the likelihood and imminence of any potential harm), the employer must seek reasonable medical judgments relying on the most current medical knowledge and/or the best available factual evidence concerning the employee.

Example: An employee with a known psychiatric disability was hospitalized for two suicide attempts, which occurred within several weeks of each other. When the employee asked to return to work, the employer allowed him to return pending an evaluation of medical reports to determine his ability to safely perform his job. The individual's therapist and psychiatrist both submitted documentation stating that he could safely perform all of his job functions. Moreover, the employee performed his job safely after his return, without reasonable accommodation. The employer, however, terminated the individual's employment after evaluating the doctor's and therapist's reports, without citing any contradictory medical or factual evidence concerning the employee's recovery. Without more evidence, this employer cannot support its determination that this individual poses a direct threat.

Finally, in addition to ethical and legal considerations, it's developmentally and educationally unsupportable to automatically withdraw students thought to be at risk of suicide. Many of those students will be struggling with a mood disorder. What they need is ongoing human connection, not prompt severance from what may be a vital channel of support.

An article in the June 2001 issue of *Psychiatric Services* (published by the American Psychiatric Association) highlights the power of human contact in suicide prevention.[105] The authors (Jerome A. Motto, M.D. and Alan G. Bostrom, Ph.D., from the University of San Francisco School of Medicine and the University of San Francisco School of Nursing) studied over 800 patients who had refused ongoing care after being hospitalized for being at risk of suicide. The patients were randomly divided into two groups. One group was contacted by letter several times a year for five years; the other received no further contact. The aim of the study was to see "if the development of a feeling of connectedness" would "exert a suicide-prevention influence."

The authors reported that:

[D]uring the period of maximum contact, year 1, and during the subsequent year, the suicide rate was significantly lower in the contact group than in the control group. It also appears that no obvious extraneous influence distorted the data—for example, age or sex differences or concealment of suicides as accidental or natural deaths.

As the frequency of contact diminished (ending in five years) so did the preventive influence. By the fourteenth year there were no differences between the contact and control groups.

Nearly a quarter of the patients who received letters expressed appreciation. Sample comments cited by the authors included:

It is a good feeling to know you are still interested," "Farewell until your next note," "After I threw the last letter out I wished I hadn't, so I was glad to get this one," "I really appreciate your persistence and concern . . ." "Your note gave me a warm, pleasant feeling. Just knowing someone cares means a lot . . ." "You will never know what your little notes mean to me. I always think someone cares about what happens to me, even if my family did kick me out. I am really grateful," and "You are the most persistent son of a bitch I've ever encountered, so you must really be sincere in your interest in me.

Motto and Bostrom cited the work of HG Morgan, who studied suicide prevention techniques used for over 600 years. Morgan concluded that "there is surely at least one common theme through the centuries it is the provision of human contact, the comfort of another concerned person, often authoritative but maybe not, conveying a message of hope consonant with the assumptions and values relevant to that particular time."[106]

Also, from an educational perspective, as Kay Redfield Jamison has observed, there is a "literary, biographical, and scientific argument for a compelling association, not to say actual overlap, between two temperaments—the artistic and the manic-depressive."[107] Although mental illnesses must not be romanticized, more than a few students at risk of suicide will exhibit high levels of creativity.[108] Others will be facing extraordinary life crises, that may later contribute to deeper understanding of themselves and others.[109] To routinely dismiss such students without careful, individualized suicide threat assessment and treatment risks dismissing some of the most thoughtful and creative students at the school. The unnecessary loss of educational opportunities for them represents a loss for the entire society.

7. HAVE ANY UNIVERSITY PROGRAMS SHOWN CONSISTENT SUCCESS IN REDUCING STUDENT SUICIDE?

Yes. The University of Illinois began a comprehensive suicide reduction program in 1984. Paul Joffe, director of Illinois' suicide-prevention program and a counselor in the University Counseling Center, reported on the program's success in a 2003 issue of *Synfax Weekly Report*:

The most appropriate evidence, which compares the rate of suicide [among University of Illinois students] at locations within Champaign County between the eight year pre-program study period with the 18 years of the program, showed a 55.4 percent reduction in the rate of suicide. To rule out the possibility that this decrease was part of a larger decrease in the rate of suicide, either nationally or at midwestern universities, these results were compared with suicide rates both nationally and at 11 peer institutions in the Big Ten. Both comparisons showed that the rate of suicide at the University of Illinois was declining at that same time rates nationally and within the Big Ten were essentially stable.[110]

Core components of the Illinois program include:

[a] *Recognizing the limits of the "invite and encourage" model.* The Illinois program began with an emphasis on contacting students who had made suicide threats or attempts in order to "invite and encourage them" to see a mental health professional. Paul Joffe reports that the results were disappointing:

> A surprising number of students emphatically denied that they had ever made a suicide threat or attempt in spite of the existence of suicide notes, eyewitnesses and other evidence to the contrary. A large number of students admitted to having been suicidal at the time of the incident but claimed to have made a complete and lasting recovery, making meeting with a social worker or psychologist unnecessary. A number of students would acquiesce to the request to make an appointment but not actually make it. Some students would schedule an appointment but not keep it. Several students attended appointments but did not inform the therapist of the recent attempt and instead focused on career issues or a problem with procrastination.
>
> A few students lied, telling their residence hall director that they were meeting with a professional when they were not. A few students met with professionals once but failed to keep a second or a third appointment. Another common phenomena was complete disappearance—students would not answer phone calls or respond to visits and literally could not be found for weeks. Despite the combined efforts of a cast of dozens, it was estimated that less than five percent of students contacted, met with a social worker or psychologist for four times.[111]

[b] *Identifying suicide as an act of violence.* The University of Illinois sets the stage for administrative as well as therapeutic interventions by regarding suicide as a form of prohibited violence. Paul Joffe summarized this perspective in an October 7, 2004 interview with the *Daily Illini:*

> While traditional psychology considers suicide an act of distress or desperation, Joffe said [the Illinois] program is unique in that it treats suicide as an act of violence. Joffe argues that just as murders

or assaults are not dismissed as acts of helplessness, neither should acts of violence against one's self.[112]

[c] *Enforcing a "mandated assessment" policy.* After the failure of the "invite and encourage" model, Illinois required any student who made a suicide threat or attempt to undergo four sessions of professional assessment. Sessions occur at weekly intervals, within days after a suicide threat or attempt, or release from the hospital. Students who fail to comply face disciplinary suspension. During the course of the assessment process:

> [T]he professional, at a minimum, would assess the student's current ideation, intent and access to means. Second, the professional would work with the student to reconstruct the circumstances, thoughts and feelings that surrounded and precipitated the original incident. Third, the professional would take a lifetime history of the student's suicidal intent and its various meanings and origins. Fourth, the professional would draw attention to the university's standard of self-welfare and the consequences for failing to adhere to it. These four issues would be addressed during each of the four sessions. Once addressed, the professional and student would be free to use the remaining time to explore issues that might have contributed to the threat or attempt and barring these, any issue of the student's choosing. The overwhelming majority of students made full use of the allotted time . . .[113]

[d] *Creating a suicide intervention team.* The Illinois team consists of mental health professionals, including a social worker. The team is authorized by the Dean of Students to adjudicate "a single standard of conduct regarding self-welfare" and to recommend sanctions for non-compliance to the Dean. The team has flexibility to respond promptly in a crisis:

> At each step of the program, the student [is] assessed for his or her ability and willingness to adhere to the standard of self-welfare . . . In especially entrenched cases involving alcohol abuse, open defiance, or fast-moving developments, special teams were convened to fashion the best response.[114]

[e] *Use of a mandated reporting system.* Student Affairs staff members are required to submit a "Suicide Incident Report Form" to the Counseling Center "whenever they [have] credible information that a student had threatened or attempted suicide." Faculty members are encouraged, but not required to do the same. Actions expected to trigger a report include "preparation of means (e.g. purchasing pills), practicing of means (e.g. holding a knife over one's wrist), [or] public statements, and attempts."[115]

The Illinois program is grounded on the philosophical premise that students have no right to threaten or inflict violence, including violence on themselves. It also assumes most students have some personal responsibility for their actions, even if they may be struggling with a mental disorder. Those views may grate against therapeutic sensibilities, but the Illinois program is showing consistent success at saving lives and *keeping students in college*.[116] Some variation of this systematic, campus-wide approach, coupled with efforts to identify students with symptoms of depression; educate faculty members and other gatekeepers about warning signs of suicide; and reduce the stigma of seeking professional help are likely to become core elements of college suicide prevention programs nationwide.[117]

8. WHAT ARE "BEST PRACTICES" IN STAFF TRAINING AND EDUCATIONAL PROGRAMMING?

Staff training and educational programming should encompass:

• fostering a campus-wide commitment to suicide prevention;

• promoting a sense of community and encouraging personal involvement in campus life;

• encouraging better mentoring and personal interaction between teachers and students;

• giving guidance to students, faculty and staff members about ways to assist students at risk of suicide;

• reducing the stigma associated with seeking professional help;

• helping students understand the nature of depression and providing depression screening;

• offering innovative treatment options, including anonymous online counseling;

• providing timely interventions to specialized groups, such as graduate and international students, or students and staff members who have recently encountered suicide, and

• identifying and reducing unnecessary social and academic pressures.

A good model for fostering a campus-wide commitment to suicide prevention can be seen in the United States Air Force suicide prevention program.[118] The Air Force program relies, in part, on statements by senior leaders sent in regular communications to all Air Force installations. One message from the Chief of Staff to unit commanders highlighted the importance of encouraging personnel to seek professional help:

> Communicate in your words and actions that it is not only acceptable, but a sign of strength, to recognize life problems and get professional help to deal with them constructively. This help may come from chaplains, mental health providers, family support centers, or other providers on-base or off-base. We must support and

protect to the full extent possible those courageous people who seek help early, before the crisis develops ... [signed] General Michael E. Ryan, Air Force Chief of Staff.[119]

Similar statements from a university president could energize staff members and highlight the ongoing importance of campus-wide suicide prevention efforts.

Colleges traditionally give high priority to promoting a sense of community. The goal is important as an end in itself and because higher levels of anxiety reported by young people (also associated with higher rates of depression) appear to be associated with "decreases in social connectedness" in American society.[120] Specific advice for institutional gatekeepers like resident advisors might include:

> One of the most important things you can do for your residents is to get to know them as individuals. Pay attention to them. Greet them. Listen to their concerns. Develop group activities designed to help students form connections with others, including faculty mentors. Pay attention to "loners" or students who seem left out. Enhanced personal connection is not a panacea for preventing suicide, but it should be an essential component of any suicide prevention program.[121]

Likewise, enhancing the traditional role of faculty members as guides and mentors can reduce student isolation and give educators more insight into what individual students are thinking and feeling.[122] The aim is not to supplant professional therapy, but to help faculty members understand the stresses students are encountering and to identify and refer students in crisis. An example of the kinds of initiatives that might be considered is a series of student mental health "information sessions" provided to University of Virginia faculty members in 2005.[123]

Faculty members should also be reminded about the impulsive nature of many suicides, and value of teaching students skills in careful decisionmaking,[124] including the decision to seek professional help when symptoms of depression arise. Reiteration in and outside the classroom that seeking appropriate help is a *mature decision making skill* may be an important factor in reducing the stigma sometimes associated with utilizing mental health services.

Key elements of the suicide prevention guidance given to faculty members can be shared with other gatekeepers, including residence advisors, student activities coordinators, and coaches, among others. At the core of the guidance might be some variation of the "LINK" program used by the Air Force:

> Look for possible concerns;
>
> Inquire about concerns;
>
> Note level of risk;
>
> Know referral resources and strategies.[125]

It's especially important to include health center physicians in on-going suicide prevention training. They need to be alert to signs of depression (e.g. lack of energy, loss of appetite, sleeplessness) and the manic depressive elements of "lovesickness"[126] and be able to ask students specific questions designed to assess suicide risk.[127]

Educational programming and screening are vital components of a suicide prevention program—and are also components of an overall risk management strategy.[128] Student participation in the design of such efforts is desirable, since student leaders usually know how to reach and influence their peers.[129] Advice given by the organization "Screening for Mental Health" includes:

- Stick to areas with heavy traffic: the student union, dining halls, large dorms. If you have the staff for it, set up more than one location.
- Most students get their news online. Make sure your event and/or your school's online screening is publicized on the college's intranet, through electronic bulletin boards or the school website's calendar.
- Send an email to faculty encouraging them to announce in-person and/or online screenings in class or offer extra credit for taking a screening. Let RA's know that screening/education events are an easy way to fulfill their floor/house event requirements.
- Make It Fun ... Dress it up with the posters, banners and flyers [available for National Depression Screening Day]. The idea is to decrease the stigma attached to mental health disorders; promote events with non-judgmental phrases like "Test Your Moods ..."[130]

College administrators and mental health professionals will also want to explore alternative treatment options, including immediate anonymous E-mail counseling. MIT, in the aftermath of the Shin suicide,[131] has been active in providing such services, including services to graduate students. According to an April 2005 article in *U.S. News and World Report*:

Today, [MIT] has a rapid-response system that allows any student to see a therapist within a day—24 hours a day, seven days a week ... and, starting soon, a Web-based suicide prevention program that offers anonymous E-mail counseling. Individual MIT [graduate] departments have made further improvements. In chemistry, eight students from each of the four departmental divisions have been trained as mediators and are available to provide a friendly ear or to direct someone to the appropriate counseling resource ... [132]

The Jed Foundation also provides anonymous online resources and screening through a program called *Ulifeline.*[133]

The attention paid to graduate students in MIT suicide prevention programs highlights the importance of providing timely interventions to specialized groups, such as graduate and international students, or students and staff members who have recently encountered suicide. Cornell University has attracted national attention in this regard by appointing special "outreach counselors" for groups "considered at heightened risk for mental health problems,"[134] including international students and Asian-American students.[135]

Finally, staff training and educational programming might also focus on the exceptional stresses reported by many college students. It's tempting, of course, to see contemporary students as over-indulged —not over-stressed. That "over-indulgence," however, seems designed to groom students for a relentlessly competitive social and economic treadmill, beginning with entry into select pre-schools and continuing throughout high school to college, graduate school, and, eventually, to America's frenetic workplace. However expensive the academic grooming process, it probably seems less pleasant to participants than observers. Some students report in this regard that they feel like perpetual "pre-beings," pre-law, pre-medicine, or pre-business—not individuals allowed to live and think in the present.[136]

The entire generation has been described by one knowledgeable observer as being on a "perfection machine" or treadmill "where they don't feel they have a choice to get off ..."[137]. No one institution is going to change this cultural phenomenon,[138] but educators can ameliorate it[139] by helping students pay more attention to the art of living, and how a good life might be defined.[140] It may also be desirable to develop less competitive grading structures[141] and to give students more time (and more creative examinations) so they may integrate and reflect upon what they've learned.[142]

9. WHAT SHOULD BE DONE AFTER A SUICIDE OCCURS?

There's surprisingly little guidance on this topic, given the extraordinary pain and disorientation felt by suicide survivors, including health care providers.[143] The following list is a starting point for elaboration and refinement on individual campuses:[144]

[a] *Staff members should be trained to treat suicide as a medical emergency* requiring the immediate combined response of medical personnel and deputized law enforcement agencies. Unless emergency assistance can be provided to the victim, the primary responsibilities of staff members on the scene are to summon appropriate help, prevent any tampering with or removal of pertinent evidence, and to assist in crowd control. Normally, a physician or other authorized person will be summoned to pronounce death.

[b] *Personal property of the victim should be secured.* Any notes or other pertinent information should be called to the immediate atten-

tion of the police. No pertinent files or records (including those maintained by college or university officials, therapists, or resident advisors) should be altered, destroyed or removed.

[c] *Witnesses or other knowledgeable persons should be called to the immediate attention of the police.* Individuals having information about the suicide should be asked to write a detailed statement.

[d] *An institutional crisis management team should be activated,* including a public information officer or other person designated to answer inquiries from the press. Immediate notification needs to be sent to designated persons on the institutional emergency contact list, including the director of the counseling or mental health center, chaplains, and legal counsel.

[e] *Standard institutional protocols should be followed for notifying next of kin after a death.* Such notification is usually undertaken by local public safety personnel and grief counselors. A designated member of the crisis management team (preferably a senior administrator) should contact next of kin promptly after notification of death has been made.

[f] *Staff members working with next of kin should receive guidance on the grieving process* in the aftermath of suicide. Commentators suggest that "survivors feel more anguish in searching for an explanation of the suicide, have higher levels of shame, and feel more rejected and betrayed than other groups."[145] There is also evidence that "[s]uicide survivors themselves have an elevated risk of suicide," and that "higher levels of depression [have been found] in the siblings of adolescent suicide victims six months after the death, and in the mothers of the victims one year afterward, compared with a control group."[146]

[g] *Individuals likely to know the victim (including friends, roommates, teammates, and teachers) should be identified and offered appropriate support.* Special attention should be paid to resident advisors, academic advisors, or other individuals who worked with the victim. First responders and other individuals who may have seen the body should also receive individualized counseling. Any effort to ban the victims' friends from responding to media inquiries is unwise and unenforceable, but persons informed about the suicide should be told about the role of the crisis management team (including arrangements by the team to notify next of kin) and the ethical responsibility to protect the privacy of the victim and the victim's family.

[h] *Any mental health professionals who worked with the victim are likely to feel "defeated, guilty, and defensive."*[147] They need emotional support from their colleagues and guidance about subsequent inquiries they are likely to encounter. They must refrain from removing, alt-

ering or modifying the victim's treatment records[148] and are obligated to respect legal and ethical obligations of confidentiality which survive the victim's death.[149] Respecting confidentiality should not preclude meeting with family members,[150] or attending the funeral. A simple, sincere statement of condolences is appropriate and desirable. Indeed, defensiveness and the absence of human feeling may be factors in fostering litigation.

[i] *A senior staff member should be assigned as an ongoing contact and resource person* to the family of the victim. Issues to be addressed include transportation to and housing on or near campus, disposition of the victims' belongings, possible tuition and fee refunds, arrangements for a memorial service (if desired), wording of press releases or obituaries, information about and support during a coroner's inquest, possible preparation of a "psychological autopsy," (with family consent)[151] and the availability of counseling for family members, including siblings. To the extent possible pertinent expenses should be borne by the institution. Follow-up communication with the family to offer moral support and understanding is often welcome.[152]

[j] *Discussions should be undertaken with local media on standards for reporting suicide.* Although the issue is not free from controversy, most experts believe suicides occur in clusters and that "[r]esearch studies over the past three decades have convincingly demonstrated that certain ways of describing suicide in the news media contribute to what behavioral scientists call 'suicide contagion.'"[153] Guidelines for appropriate reporting about suicide include the observations that:

> Dramatizing the impact of suicide through descriptions and pictures of grieving relatives, teachers or classmates or community expressions of grief may encourage potential victims to see suicide as a way of getting attention or as a form of retaliation against others ... Using adolescents on TV or in print media to tell the stories of their suicide attempts may be harmful to the adolescents themselves or may encourage other vulnerable young people to seek attention in this way.[154]

10. WHAT IS THE ROLE OF COLLEGE AND UNIVERSITY LEGAL COUNSEL?

Lawyers have the reputation of being reflexively risk adverse, sometimes to the point of sabotaging the core mission of the company or institution they represent. The stereotype will have less force if lawyers differentiate between *assessing* legal risk (one of their primary responsibilities) and *deciding what legal risks to take* (the responsibility of senior administrators). Keeping this distinction in mind is especially important in a campus climate of shared governance and collegiality.

The assessment of legal risk involves doing more than following the latest legal fads. Some consultants and practitioners (usually with honorable intentions) make a good living creating annual stampedes among frightened administrators who are sometimes induced to make hasty policy changes based upon inflammatory press reports, self-interested legal analysis by national advocacy groups, and questionable lower court decisions which may not survive an appeal.

Risk assessment is both a science and an art. It entails quantitative measures,[155] analysis of key precedents[156] and careful reading of national social and political trends (like the growing role of baby boomer parents in the lives of their adult children). Risk assessment also involves balancing one risk against another—such as the largely undefined risk of liability for student suicide, against the more established risk of prematurely dismissing or withdrawing students in violation of the state and federal disability laws.

Lawyers can and should use their risk assessment skills to make reasoned predictions, but doing so requires a measure of humility, openly expressed. Some clients, misunderstanding the "evolutionary" nature of the law (e.g., different jurisdictions test multiple, often contradictory approaches to similar problems) may demand simple answers and definitive forecasts. Beyond unfamiliarity with the law, such demands may also reflect a desire to transfer decision making authority on controversial issues to professionals with "unchallengeable" technical expertise. College and university attorneys will be tempted to assume this role, but doing so pushes them beyond the limits of their knowledge and stifles the creativity, humanity, and wisdom that can arise when multiple policy opinions are heard and debated.

Lawyers who encourage the traits of humility, creativity, humanity and wisdom in institutional management merit the title "counselor" in the fullest sense of that word. They know, in the context of student suicide, that automatic rules and defensive policies create precisely the kind of antagonism and bitterness that invites litigation.[157] They also know that institutions like colleges and universities earn respect and social support by endeavoring to fulfill their educational mission, not by finding expeditious ways of dismissing promising, but troubled students.[158]

Lawyers as "counselors" also have an important role in drawing insight from cases and developing pertinent interventions. For example, a recurring pattern in recent college student suicide litigation is the failure of gatekeepers like resident advisors to treat known suicide threats and attempts as full-blown emergencies. Counsel can call such patterns to the attention of administrators and mental health professionals, helping to fashion new protocols and guidelines. Perhaps more than most other lawyers, college and university attorneys use legal knowledge to foster collaboration and teamwork among a broad array of staff members from different disciplines and specialities. The aim is not to sit on high reviewing the work of others, but to *anticipate* legal risks (realistically defined) and to help colleagues find practical solutions, consistent with institutional goals and values.

Finally, there remains the role of counsel as mediator and peacemaker. An aura of aggressive certitude may reassure clients in the midst of litigation, but it isn't a suitable quality for every occasion. The best course for individuals and institutions is to listen carefully to criticism and grievances, correcting obvious mistakes and making reasoned exceptions to established policies. Indeed, one of the greatest services a lawyer can give a client is to support the client's sound ethical instinct to offer an injured party a sincere and justified apology.[159] The law is grounded on many competing aims and values, but the greatest of all is reciprocity.

Notes

1. "Suicide: Fact Sheet," Centers for Disease Control and Prevention (CDC), July 26, 2004. Available at http://www.cdc.gov/ncipc/factsheets/suifacts.htm. (Last viewed May 31, 2005). See also National Youth Violence Prevention Resource Center (sponsored by the CDC), "Teen Suicides Dip 25 Percent" (citing a CDC study reported under the same title in the June 11, 2004 *Atlanta Constitution*).

2. National Center for Policy Analysis, "U.S. Youth Suicide Rates Down—But Still High," *Daily Policy Digest*, Friday, December 14, 2001.

3. National Youth Violence Prevention Resource Center (developed by the CDC), "Youth Suicide Fact Sheet," 2001.

4. National Institute of Mental Health, "Suicide Facts and Statistics," last viewed May 30, 2005 at: http://www.nimh.nih.gov/suicideprevention/suifact.cfm

5. See Paul Joffe, (director of the University of Illinois suicide-prevention program), "The Illinois Plan, Part I," *Synfax Weekly Report* 03.41 (October, 2003): "After decades of debate over whether the rate of suicide was higher or lower among college-attending young adults ... [multiple researchers have] convincingly established the rate to be roughly half the rate for young adults in the general population." Pertinent trends can be tracked at several online sources, including the National Institute for Mental Health (http://www.nimh.nih.gov/) (see suicide rates for 15- to 24-year-olds) and the Jed Foundation (http://jedfoundation.org/suicide.php) (see suicide rates for college students).

6. See generally David M.. Cutler, Edward L. Glaeser, and Karen E. Norberg, "Explaining the Rise in Youth Suicide," May 2000, National Bureau of Economic Research, Working Paper 7713, p. 28.

7. Anne McGrath, "Curing campus blues" *U.S. New and World Report online edition*, November 1, 2004 (interview with Richard Kadison, chief of Harvard University mental health service, co-author of *College of the Overwhelmed: The Campus Mental Health Crisis and What to Do About It* (Jossey-Bass, 2004). See also Mary Duenwald "The Consumer: The Dorms May Be Great, but How's the Counseling?" *New York Times online edition*, October 26, 2004. Comparable data were released in November 2004 by the National College Health Assessment survey, available at: http://www.acha.org/projects_programs/assessment.cfm (Viewed May 30, 2005).

8. Deborah Sontag "Who Was Responsible For Elizabeth Shin?" *The New York Times Sunday Magazine* (online edition) April 28, 2002.

9. Harvard Economists and NBER researchers David M.. Cutler, Edward L. Glaeser, and Karen E. Norberg, (supra, note 6) state that: "[w]e find that to the extent we can explain the rise in youth suicide over time, the most important aggregate variable explaining this change seems to be the increased share of youths living in homes with a divorced parent," p. 6.

10. Editorial, *The British Journal of Psychiatry*, (2001) 178: 494-496.

11. An abridged version of the "Practice Guideline for the Assessment and Treatment of Patients With Suicidal Behaviors" is available at the American Psychiatric Association website: http://www.psych.org/research/ (*last viewed May 30, 2005*).

12. William Kanapaux, "Guideline to Aid Treatment of Suicidal Behavior," *Psychiatric Times* (July 2004) 21:8, 1,3.

13. Kay Redfield Jamison, *Night Falls Fast: Understanding Suicide*, (Knoph 1999), p. 189.

14. See "Antidepressant Use By U.S. Adults Soars," *Washington Post* December 3, 2004, p.A15 (including editor's correction in online edition):

> One in 10 American women takes an antidepressant drug such as Prozac, Paxil or Zoloft, and the use of such drugs by all adults has nearly tripled in the last decade, according to the latest figures on American health released yesterday by the federal government ... The number of children getting psychiatric drugs also soared. In 2002, about 6 percent of doctor's office visits by children involved prescriptions for antidepressants, and about 14 percent of office visits by boys involved prescriptions for stimulant drugs ... Stimulant drugs are usually used to treat attention deficit disorder.

15. The Jed Foundation Website is available at http://jedfoundation.org/index.php. The cited reference is at http://jedfoundation.org/articles/Suicide Statistics.pdf. (*Last viewed May 30, 2005*).

16. Kay Redfield Jamison, *supra*, note 13: "[F]amily, twin and adoption studies make a strong case for a strong genetic influence on suicide ... Genes are, of course, only a part of the tangle of suicide, but their collision with psychological and environmental elements can prove ... to be the difference between life and death" p. 172.

17. Jamison, *supra*, note 13, p. 189: "[S]uicidal patients, in addition to being more impulsive, are also more likely to commit violent or aggressive acts than non-suicidal patients. In one English study, those who actually killed themselves were three times more likely to have had a history of violent behavior then the individuals matched with them for age, gender, and social class."

Readers should be reminded, of course, that the general correlation between suicide and other forms of violence does not enable mental health professionals to predict the future behavior of specific individuals. Violence toward others remains as unpredictable as violence toward self. See, generally, the American Psychiatric Association "Statement on Prediction of Dangerousness" available in December 2004 at the APA website.

The Statement says that:

> [P]sychiatrists have no special knowledge or ability with which to predict dangerous behavior. Studies have shown that even with patients in which there is a history of violent acts, predictions of future violence will be wrong for two out of every three patients.

See also our analysis of the MacArthur Study of Mental Disorder and Violence in *Synfax Weekly Report:* Andrew Flack and Gary Pavela "Can violence be predicted," 02.59, p. 3088 (week of December 9, 2002). We conclude that: "[a]lthough violence prediction techniques have improved since the time when unstructured clinical opinion reigned, there's little on the research horizon that indicates researchers will ever find a way to predict future behavior with precision."

18. Jamison, *supra*, note 13, p. 206-207: "The seasonal variation in suicide is one of the robust and consistent findings in the research literature . . . The peak months for suicide were, with rare exceptions, in the late spring and summer. Likewise, the lowest rates were always found in the winter months."

19. Jamison, *supra*, note 13, p. 277-278: "The tendency for suicide to incite imitation, especially if the death is highly publicized or romanticized, is persistent." See our response to question nine, *infra*.

20. American Psychiatric Association "Assessing and Treating Suicidal Behaviors: A Quick Reference Guide," *supra*, note 11.

21. See Kanapaux, *supra*, note 12: "According to Douglas G. Jacobs, M.D., '[n]one of the scales that are out there are specific enough or sensitive enough for general clinical usage. Suicide assessment still is left to the judgment of the psychiatrist based upon a comprehensive psychiatric examination, a review of current and past treatment, and a detailed inquiry into suicidal thinking and behavior.'"

22. See *Bogust v. Iverson*, 102 N.W.2d 228 (Wisconsin, 1960) (non-therapist college advisor had no duty to prevent student suicide); *Nally v. Grace Community Church*, 763 P.2d 948 (Cal., 1988) (non-therapist counselors had no duty to prevent suicide); *Donaldson v. Young Women's Christian Association of Duluth*, 539 N.W.2d 789 (Minn., 1995) (no special relationship between YWCA and guest who committed suicide); and *Lee v. Corregedore*, 925 P.2d 324 (Haw. 1996) (non-therapist Veterans' Services counselor had no duty to prevent client's suicide in an outpatient setting). For views on the possible direction of the law see Peter Lake and Nancy Tribbensee, "The Emerging Crisis of College Student Suicide: Law and Policy Responses to Serious Forms of Self-Inflicted Injury," 32 *Stetson Law Review* 125 (2002), and Ann Franke (vice president for education and risk management at United Educators Insurance), "When Students Kill Themselves, Colleges May Get the Blame," *Chronicle of Higher Education*, June 25, 2004, p. B18.

23. *Wallace v. Broyles*, 961 S. W. 2d 712 (Ark. 1998).

24. See, generally, Robert Simon "Patient Suicide and Litigation," *Psychiatric Times* May 2004, p. 18-21. Simon, clinical professor of psychiatry at the Georgetown University School of Medicine, is the author of *Assessing and Managing Suicide Risk: Guidelines for Clinically Based Risk Management* (American Psychiatric Publishing, 2004). In his *Psychiatric Times* article Simon noted that although most suicide liability lawsuits against mental health professionals involve inpatient treatment or discharge decisions, "exposure of out-patient psychiatrists to legal liability has significantly increased." Simon found, however that psychiatrists prevail "[i]n eight out of every 10 claims taken to trial." *Supra*, p, 21.

25. *Jain v. State of Iowa* 617 N.W. 2d 293, 300 (Iowa, 2000). See *Synfax Weekly Report* "Liability for suicide: Failure to notify parents of suicide threats, " 00.42, week of December 4, 2000, p. 1049.

26. *Jain, supra*, p 299-300.

27. *Jain, supra*, p 299.

28. Ann Franke, *supra* n. 22 reports that suicide liability lawsuits are "growing in frequency," with "about 10 [pending] nationwide," p. B18.

29. *Schieszler v. Ferrum College* 236 F. Supp. 2d 602, 609, (W.D. Va. 2002)

30. *Shin v. MIT* Superior Court Civil Action No. 02-0403, Middlesex, ss, Memorandum of Decision and Order on Defendants' Motions for Summary Judgment.

31. *Eisel v. Board of Education of Montgomery County* 597 A.2d 447 (Md. 1991). See review and commentary in *Synfax Weekly Report* "Preventing suicide" 00.43, week of December 11, 2000, p. 1052.

32. Eisel, *supra.*

33. Associated Press story dated October 22, 2004. Abstract available (by search function) at: http://www.safeyouth.org/scripts/index.asp *(last viewed May 30, 2005).*

34. See Richard Fossey and Perry Zirkel, "Liability for Student Suicide in the Wake of Eisel," 10 *Texas Wesleyan University Law Review* 403 (2004).

35. See *Nally v. Grace Community Church* (1988), *supra* n. 22.

> Plaintiffs failed to persuade us that the duty to prevent suicide (here-tofore imposed only on psychiatrists and hospitals while caring for a suicidal patient) or the general professional duty of care (heretofore imposed only on psychiatrists when treating a mentally disturbed patient) should be extended to a nontherapist counselor who offers counseling to a potentially suicidal person on secular or spiritual matters.

36. See the suicide prevention training module for Resident Advisors in the appendix.

37. Nor should staff members accept student assurances that they're "feeling better." Kay Redfield Jamison, *(supra,* n. 13) found that "more than half the patients who killed themselves in psychiatric hospitals had been described by nursing or medical staff, just before their suicides, as 'clinically improved' or 'improving,'" p.152.

38. Robert Simon, *Assessing and Managing Suicide Risk: Guidelines for Clinically Based Risk Management* (American Psychiatric Publishing, 2004), p. 80-81.

39. *Shin v. MIT supra,* n. 30.

40. *Kockelman v. Segal* 61 Cal App. 4th 491, 71 Cal. Rptr. 2d 552 (1998); See also *Bellah v. Greenson* 81 Cal. App. 3d 614, 619, 146 Cal. Rptr 535, 538 (1978) ("A psychiatrist who knows that his patient is likely to attempt suicide has a duty to take preventive measures").

41. *Kockelman supra,* 71 Cal Rptr. 2d at 560.

42. *Jacoves v. United Merchandising Corp,* 9 Cal App. 4th 88, 11 Cal. Rptr. 2d 468 (1992).

43. *Supra,* 11 Cal. Rptr. 2d at 478.

44. Simon, *supra,* n. 38 p, 37.

45. Jamison, *supra,* n. 13, p. 269.

46. Simon, *supra,* note 38.

47. Simon, *supra,* note 38, p. 183.

48. See, generally, Douglas G. Jacobs, MD Editor *The Harvard Medical School Guide to Suicide Assessment and Intervention,* Jossey-Bass (1999).

49. Douglas Jacobs and Margaret Brewer,"Treating Patients with Suicidal Behaviors," *Psychiatric Annals,* May 2004; last viewed on May 30, 2005 at http://www.stopasuicide.org/images/APASuicideGuidelinesReviewArticle.pdf

50. Douglas Jacobs and Margaret Brewer, *supra.*

51. Simon, *supra,* note 38, p. 194-5.

52. See, generally, Simon, *supra,* note 38, p. 194.

53. Jeffrey Stovall and Frank Domino, "Approaching the Suicidal Patient," *American Family Physician,* Vol 68, November 1, 2003. Viewed February 17, 2005 at http://www.aafp.org/afp/20031101/1814.pdf.

54. See *Schieszler v. Ferrum College,* 236 F. Supp. 2d 602, 609 (W.D. Va. 2002).

The defendants [college officials] knew that Frentzel had sent other communications, to his girlfriend and to another friend, suggesting that he intended to kill himself. After Frentzel was found alone in his room with bruises on his head, the defendants required Frentzel to sign a statement that he would not hurt himself. This last fact, more than any other, indicates that the defendants believed Frentzel was likely to harm himself. Based on these alleged facts, a trier of fact could conclude that there was "an imminent probability" that Frentzel would try to hurt himself, and that the defendants had notice of this specific harm. Thus, I find that the plaintiff has alleged sufficient facts to support her claim that a special relationship existed between Frentzel and defendants giving rise to a duty to protect Frentzel from the foreseeable danger that he would hurt himself.

55. Kay Redfield Jamison, *Supra,* n.13, p. 269. Likewise, Simon cites research showing that "58% of outpatients who committed suicide has seen a psychiatrist the prior week." *Supra,* n. 38, p. 92.

56. Demand for college mental health services is high. Institutions that provide quality care will have a competitive advantage. The ultimate cost (factoring in suitable insurance coverage required of all students), should be substantially less than other features of contemporary campus life, such as free music downloading, saunas, steam rooms, and cable television in the residence halls.

57. Simon, *supra,* n. 38, p. 80.

58. *Supra,* p. 92.

59. *Klein v. Solomon* 713 A.2d 764 (R.I., 1998).

60. *Supra,* at 765, 766.

61. *Supra* at 766.

62. See William Kanapaux, "Guideline to Aid Treatment of Suicidal Behavior," *Psychiatric Times,* July 2004, viewed February 24, 2005 at http://www.psychiatric times.com/p040701a.html

[A] high-risk patient usually requires hospital treatment; however, there are always exceptions, such as if a patient is well known to the psychiatrist and has a supportive family. Likewise, a patient with moderate risk might need to be hospitalized due to clinical circumstances.

63. Simon, *supra,* n. 38 states that "[m]alpractice suits have been filed against psychiatrists alleging failure to involuntarily hospitalize patients at risk of suicide. This type of suit is far more common than a lawsuit against a therapist for committing a patient" p. 95.

64. William Styron, *Darkness Visible,* (Vintage, 1992), p. 68-69.

65. See *Shin v. MIT, supra* n. 30, p. 16:

The Plaintiffs' argue that MIT medical professionals individually and collectively failed to coordinate Elizabeth's care. As a "treatment team" the professionals failed to secure Elizabeth's short term safety in response to Elizabeth's suicide plan in the morning hours of April 10. During the "deans and psychs" meeting on the morning of April 10, plans to assist Elizabeth were discussed, however, an immediate response to Elizabeth's escalating threats to commit suicide were not formulated. By not formulating and enacting an immediate plan to respond to Elizabeth's escalating threats to commit suicide, the plaintiffs have put forth sufficient evidence of a genuine issue of material fact as to whether the MIT medical professionals were grossly negligent in their treatment of Elizabeth.

66. See "Antidepressant Seen as Effective in Treatment of Adolescents" June 2, 2004 *New York Times:*

[A] landmark government-financed study has found that Prozac helps teenagers overcome depression far better than talk therapy. But a combination of the two treatments, the study found, produced the best result.

Mental health professionals, of course, will also be taking cognizance of some studies showing higher rates of suicidal thinking or behavior among adolescents taking certain anti-depressants. Pertinent guidance from the National Institute of Mental Health is available at: http://www.nimh.nih.gov/healthinformation/antidepressant_child.cfm. *(Last viewed on May 30, 2005.)*

67. See Donna Wirshing, et. al., "Medicolegal Considerations in the Treatment of Psychoses with Second Generation Antipsychotics," *Psychiatric Times*, December, 2004, p. 22, 24: "A good relationship with patients and their families is key to preventing an adversarial relationship from developing, even in the event of the worst possible outcomes."

68. Robert I. Simon, "Patient Suicide and Litigation," *Psychiatric Times*, May 2004, p. 18, 21.

69. The legal privilege is grounded on ethical standards established by the mental health professions. See, e.g. "The Principles of Medical Ethics with Annotations Especially Applicable to Psychiatry" (American Psychiatric Association, 2001) viewed March 18, 2005 at: http:www.ama-assn.org/ama/pub/category/13351.html.

Psychiatric records, including even the identification of a person as a patient, must be protected with extreme care. Confidentiality is essential to psychiatric treatment. This is based in part on the special nature of psychiatric therapy as well as on the traditional ethical relationship between physician and patient. Growing concern regarding the civil rights of patients and the possible adverse effects of computerization, duplication equipment, and data banks makes the dissemination of confidential information an increasing hazard.

For a review of pertinent case law see *Lee v. Corregedore* 925 P.2d 324, 337 (1996).

"Were it not for the assurance of confidentiality in the counselor-client relationship, many in need of counseling would be reluctant to even seek counseling, and those who do seek counseling under such circumstances would probably be deterred from fully disclosing their problems to their counselors ... Furthermore, there is authority suggesting that health care workers can be subject to civil liability by disclosing confidential information to third parties ... For example ... [in] *Watts v. Cumberland County Hospital System, Inc* ... 330 S.E.2d 242, 248-50 (1985) ... the court wrote that:

> Various theories have been suggested as a basis for the cause of action, including invasion of privacy, breach of implied contract, breach of fiduciary duty or duty of confidentiality, and medical malpractice. Courts considering the issue have not agreed upon the proper characterization of the cause of action and, in some cases, have held that liability may be imposed under more than one theory.

[See] ... *Alberts v. Devine*, 479 N.E.2d 113, 120 (Mass. 1985) (holding that a duty of confidentiality arises from the psychiatrist-patient relationship "and that a violation of that duty, resulting in damages, gives rise to a cause of action sounding in tort against the physician"), *cert. denied, Caroll v. Alberts*, 474 U.S. 1013 (1985); *Vassiliades v. Garfinckel's, Brooks Bros.*, 492 A.2d 580, 592 (D.C. 1985) ("We hold that the breach of a physician-patient relationship [by disclosing confidential information] is an actionable tort."); *MacDonald v. Clinger*, 446 N.Y.S.2d 801, 802 (N.Y. App. Div. 1982) (holding that a psychiatrist's wrongful disclosure of confidential information to a patient's wife "[wa]s a breach of the fiduciary duty of confidentiality and g[ave] rise to a cause of action sounding in tort") ... *Hammonds v. Aetna Casualty & Surety Co.*, 243 F.Supp. 793, 802 (N.D. Ohio 1965) ("The unauthorized revelation of medical secrets, or any confidential communication given in the course of treatment, is tortious conduct which may be the basis for an action in damages."). Requiring counselors to breach counselor-client confidentiality would force counselors to incur a greater risk of civil liability, which, in turn, might discourage people from serving as counselors. Confidentiality, of course, is not absolute. See note 88, *infra*.

70. FERPA regulations can be found at 34 CFR Part 99, available online at: http://www.ed.gov/policy/gen/reg/ferpa/index.html

A question and answer document prepared by the U.S. Department of Education is available online at: http://www.ed.gov/policy/gen/guid/fpco/faq.html-q1

Question and Answer five contains the following analysis:

Q. *If I am a parent of a college student, do I have the right to see my child's education records, especially if I pay the bill?*

A. [T]he rights under FERPA transfer from the parents to the student, once the student turns 18 years old or enters a postsecondary institution at any age. However, although the rights under FERPA have now transferred to the student, a school may disclose information from an "eligible student's" education records to the parents of the student, without the student's consent, if the student is a dependent for tax purposes. Neither the age of the student nor the parent's status as a custodial parent is relevant. If a student is claimed as a dependent by either parent for tax purposes, then either parent may have access under this provision. (34 CFR §99.31(a)(8).)

71. The FERPA emergency exception is defined at 34 CFR §99.31

§99.31 Under what conditions is prior consent not required to disclose information?

(a) An educational agency or institution may disclose personally identifiable information from an education record of a student without the consent required by §99.30 if the disclosure meets one or more of the following conditions . . .

10) The disclosure is in connection with a health or safety emergency, under the conditions described in §99.36.

* * *

§99.36 What conditions apply to disclosure of information in health and safety emergencies?

(a) An educational agency or institution may disclose personally identifiable information from an education record to appropriate parties in connection with an emergency if knowledge of the information is necessary to protect the health or safety of the student or other individuals.

(b) Nothing in the Act or this part shall prevent an educational agency or institution from

(1) Including in the education records of a student appropriate information concerning disciplinary action taken against the student for conduct that posed a significant risk to the safety or well-being of that student, other students, or other members of the school community;

(2) Disclosing appropriate information maintained under paragraph (b)(1) of this section to teachers and school officials within the agency or institution who the agency or institution has determined have legitimate educational interests in the behavior of the student; or

(3) Disclosing appropriate information maintained under paragraph (b)(1) of this section to teachers and school officials in other schools who have been determined to have legitimate educational interests in the behavior of the student.

(c) Paragraphs (a) and (b) of this section will be strictly construed.

72. 34 CFR Part 99.7

73. Language in this section is drawn from my 2002 article "The Student-university-parent partnership" in *Synfax Weekly Report* 02.6, p. 2080, (week of February 11, 2002).

74. *Washington Post* "Adolescence: Not Just for Kids." (online edition), January 2, 2002.

75. *Ibid.*

76. *Ibid.*

77. Neil Howe and William Strauss, *Millennials Rising* (Vintage, 2000).

78. *Ibid*, authors' commentary at www.millennialsrising.com/aboutbook.shtml

79. See Gary Pavela, "Today's College Students Need Both Freedom and Structure," July 29, 1992 *Chronicle of Higher Education*. We suggested that traditional age students might be defined as "Post-Adolescent Pre-Adults."

Most parents have similar views. According to an article in the January 6, 2005 *Wall Street Journal* (Jeff Zaslow, "The Coddling Crisis: Why Americans Think Adulthood Begins at Age 26," online edition) "[a] 2003 poll by the University of Chicago's National Opinion Research Center found that most Americans think adulthood begins at about age 26."

80. See Stuart Silverstein "Colleges Are Learning to Hold Parents' Hands," *Los Angeles Times*, November 28, 2004 (online edition):

> [N]ine out of 10 four-year campuses offer special orientations for parents. And about 70% of four-year schools have at least one staffer working full-time or nearly full-time with parents, according to a survey of 607 U.S. schools by the nonprofit advocacy group College Parents of America.

81. Cultural misunderstanding about the scope of parental notification appears to have been a factor in the *Shin* and *Jain* cases, *supra*, notes 8, 25 and 30.

82. Eileen McNamara, "Parents Were Last to Know," January 30, 2002 *Boston Globe*, online edition.

83. *Ibid.*

84. *Supra*, n. 8.

85. Although liability risk for parental notification is small (especially outside the context of privileged communications), we share Ann H. Franke's view (*supra*, note 22) that "[s]ometimes it just comes down to picking your lawsuit. A student's suit for invasion of privacy is, by most any reckoning, preferable to a suit preferable over a suicide."

86. See note 69, *supra*.

87. See *Lee v. Corregedore* 925 P.2d 324, (Haw. 1996).

88. See Section IV (8) of the "The Principles of Medical Ethics with Annotations Especially Applicable to Psychiatry," *supra*, n. 66:

> Psychiatrists at times may find it necessary, in order to protect the patient or the community from imminent danger, to reveal confidential information disclosed by the patient.

89. Simon, *supra*, n. 38, p. 38.

90. I am indebted to Harvard Medical School psychiatrist George H. Vaillant for this perspective. In his book *Adaptation to Life* (Little, Brown, 1977) (reporting on the Grant Study of Adult Development). Vaillant wrote that "it is not stress that kills us . . . It is affective adaptation to stress that permits us to live" (p. 374). Educators afraid of lawsuits, unfavorable publicity, or the expense of adequately funding a counseling center may try to remove troubled students from "stressful" environments. Most students, however, don't need to be protected from stress; they need to learn how to *use* and *manage* stress. See the commentary in n. 109.

91. A comparable perspective can be found in a rising chorus of protests from federal judges who object to legislation (consistently favored by Republican Congressional majorities) reducing or eliminating flexibility in imposing prison sentences. A story in the July 08, 2003 *Christian Science Monitor* ("Federal judges rebel over limits to sentencing power") (online edition) reports that:

From Washington to California, normally reticent judges at virtually all federal levels are chafing at the guidelines that, among other things, eliminate flexibility in setting jail terms for whole categories of crimes ... The protests aren't coming from just a few disgruntled liberal judges, either. William Rehnquist, the [late] chief justice of the US Supreme Court, has said he believes the changes go too far.

Federal judges know that human behavior comes in many shades of gray, reflecting the convergence of unique events and personalities. Creating general behavioral guidelines or standards is a worthy goal, both to structure rational decision making and to promote consistency. Consistency, however, should not be confused with *uniformity*. Mandatory "one size fits all" outcomes may have great appeal in the abstract, but they don't comport with the judgment and experience of those who see real people in real courtrooms.

92. "Counseling at Phillips, and Its Consequences" *New York Times* July 9, 2003 (online edition).

93. *Ibid*

94. *Ibid*

95. See, generally, *Carr v. St. John's University* 231 N.Y.S.2d 410, 413 (N.Y. App. Div.1962), aff'd, 187 N.E.2d 18 (N.Y. 1962):

When a student is duly admitted by a private university ... there is an implied contract between the student and the university that, if he complies with the terms prescribed by the university, he will obtain the degree which he sought. The university cannot take the student's money, allow him to remain and waste his time in whole or in part ... and then arbitrarily expel him ...

See also *Johnson v. Lincoln Christian College*, 501 N.E.2d 1380, 1384 (Ill. App. Ct.1986), appeal denied, 508 N.E.2d 729 (Ill. 1987) "a college 'may not act maliciously or in bad faith by arbitrarily and capriciously refusing to award a degree to a student who fulfills its degree requirement[s]'" (quoting *Tanner v.Board of Trustees of Univ. of Illinois*, 363 N.E.2d 208, 209-10 (Ill. App. Ct. 1977).

96. 42 U.S.C. §12101 et seq (ADA) and 29 U.S.C. §794 (Section 504). An OCR question and answer document on Section 504 is available at: http://www.ed.gov/about/offices/list/ocr/504faq.html–introduction

97. See, for example, pertinent language in *Dixon v. Alabama* 294 F.2d 150 (5th Cir., 1961): Turning then to the nature of the governmental power to expel the plaintiffs, it must be conceded, as was held by the district court, that that power is not unlimited and cannot be arbitrarily exercised ... [T]here must be some reasonable and constitutional ground for expulsion or the courts would have a duty to require reinstatement. The possibility of arbitrary action is not excluded by the existence of reasonable regulations. There may be arbitrary application of the rule to the facts of a particular case.

98. OCR letter ruling: Woodbury University (Docket Number 09-00-2079; June 29, 2001).

99. *Ibid*

100. Jamison, *Supra*, n.13, p. 100 has written in this regard that:

> Study after study in Europe, the United States, Australia, and Asia has shown the unequivocal presence of severe psychopathology in those who die by their own hand; indeed, in all the major investigations to date, 90 to 95 percent of the people who committed suicide had a diagnosable psychiatric illness. High rates of psychopathology have also been found in those who make serious suicide attempts.

101. See pertinent discussion of the "being regarded as having" provision of the ADA in part IV of *Sutton v. United Airlines, Inc.*, 527 U.S. 471, 489 (1999) (nearsighted pilots who could fully correct their visual impairments were not "disabled" under the ADA). The Court concluded that "[b]ecause petitioners have not alleged, and cannot demonstrate, that respondent's vision requirement reflects a belief that petitioners' vision substantially limits them, we agree with the decision of the Court of Appeals affirming the dismissal of petitioners' claim that they are regarded as disabled."

The Court in *Sutton* provided a pertinent example, applicable, (among many possibilities) to a student with bi-polar disorder who might be taking pertinent medication: "[O]ne whose high blood pressure is 'cured' by medication may be regarded as disabled by a covered entity, and thus disabled under [the ADA definition]," *id* at 488.

102. See *Thomas v. Davidson Academy*, 846 F. Supp. 611, 618 (M.D. Tenn. 1994). A federal district court in Tennessee reinstated a disabled private school student expelled for becoming "agitated" and "noncooperative" The Court observed that:

> [The principal] stated that he expected exactly the same attitude from [the dismissed student] as from any other Davidson Academy student. The Court cautions that blind adherence to policies and standards resulting in a failure to accommodate a person with a disability is precisely what the Americans with Disabilities Act of 1990 and the Rehabilitation Act of 1973 are intended to prevent ...

103. See our answer to question two.

104. *Supra*, n. 96.

105. Jerome A. Motto, M.D. and Alan G. Bostrom, Ph.D., "A Randomized Controlled Trial of Postcrisis Suicide Prevention," *Psychiatric Services* 52:828-833. The article is available online at: http://www.cci.scot.nhs.uk/cci/files/motto_and_bostrom_2001.pdf *(Last viewed May 30, 2005).*

106. HG Morgan, "Suicide and its prevention," *Journal of the Royal Society of Medicine*, 82:637, 1989. Cited in Motto and Bostrom, *supra*.

107. Kay Redfield Jamison, *Touched by Fire: Manic Depressive Illness and Artistic Temperament* (Free Press, 1998), p. 5. See also an interview with Dr. Kay Redfield Jamison, "Live from Lincoln Center," The New York Philharmonic with Kurt Masur and Sarah Chang, March 3, 1998, available at: http://www.pbs.org/lflc/backstage/march3/jamison.htm–romantic. See also n. 109, *infra*.

108. See editorial: "Of the Muse and Moods Mundane," and J. Schildkraut, et. al. "Mood and Muse in Modern Art, II: Depressive Disorders, Spirituality, and Early Deaths in the Abstract Expressionist Artists of the New York School," *The American Journal of Psychiatry*, April 1994, p. 477.

109. The critical role of certain crises—and the need to fully "live" them—is also an important theme in the late Erik Erikson's work. He wrote in *Young Man Luther* (Norton, 1962, pgs. 261-262) that:

> [R]eligiously and artistically creative men often seem to be suffering from a barely compensated psychosis, and yet later prove superhumanly

gifted in conveying a total meaning for man's life . . . [There are also instances when] malignant disturbances in late adolescence often display precocious wisdom . . . The chosen [youth] extends the problem of his identity to the borders of existence in the known universe [while] other human beings . . . adopt and fulfill the departmentalized identities which they find prepared in their communities . . .

For a similar perspective, see Joli Jenson, "Let's Not Medicate Away Student Angst," *Chronicle of Higher Education,* June 13, 2003 (online edition) and George E. Vaillant's *Adaptation to Life* (Little, Brown, 1977). Vaillant observed that:

Understanding a differentiated hierarchy of defenses also allows us, even in the maelstrom of stress and emergency, to be helpful to others in a more rational manner. We should respect the mature defenses and learn to admire and nourish them. Stoicism, altruism, and artistic creativity should rarely be interfered with (p. 371).

See also Joshua Wolf Shenk "Lincoln's Great Depression," *The Atlantic,* October 2005, p. 52-68. Shenk wrote that:

Whatever greatness Lincoln achieved cannot be explained as a triumph over personal suffering. Rather, it must be accounted an outgrowth of the same system that produced that suffering. This is a story not of transformation but of integration. Lincoln didn't do great work because he solved the problem of his melancholy; the problem of his melancholy was all the more fuel for the fire of his great work (p. 68).

See additional commentary in n. 90 and 107.

110. Paul Joffe, "The Illinois plan, part II," *Synfax Weekly Report* 03.42, Week of November 10, 2003, p. 3199.

111. *Ibid,* p. 3198.

112. "Suicide prevention program takes a new approach, works to fight violence against self," University of Illinois *Daily Illini* October 7, 2004 (online edition viewed on May 15, 2005). The University of Iowa has also developed a disciplinary response to student suicide attempts. See "Suicide Attempts and Parental Notification: Choices and Consequences for Administrators" paper presented at the 2005 Association for Student Judicial Affairs Annual Conference by Thomas Baker and Debra Wood, p. 22:

After one incident of serious self-destructive behavior, a student ordinarily will be placed on probation and permitted to enroll in school following his or her release from the hospital. The student is told in writing of the likely consequences of a subsequent act of self-destructive behavior on campus. As with any student on disciplinary probation, a second violation ordinarily results in housing eviction or a suspension from classes, or both.

113. *Ibid,* n. 110, p. 3199.

114. *Ibid,* p. 3198.

115. *Ibid,* p. 3198.

116. See Paul Joffe's paper, "An Empirically Supported Program to Prevent Suicide," delivered at the Twenty-Fourth Annual National Conference on Law and Higher Education in Clearwater Beach, Florida. Joffe (Director of Illinois' suicide prevention program) wrote that:

[T]he [University of Illinois Suicide Prevention] Team has never received a report that a student withdrew from school to avoid having to participate in the assessment process. Paradoxically, while the prevention program is based on the leverage of withdrawing students if they fail to comply, the program strongly advocated continued enrollment following even a serious suicide attempt. The Team responded to all situations with the assumption that students would continue with their studies. Over the course of the 18 years of the program, only one student was withdrawn by recommendation of the team . . . She successfully petitioned to return in the Spring Semester and returned to school three months after her withdrawal. She graduated two years later with high honors and without having been the subject of an additional suicide incident report (p. 20).

117. Education and outreach components of the Illinois suicide prevention program can be found at the University's Counseling Center web site: http://www.couns.uiuc.edu/HelpPreventSuicide.html (*Viewed May 15, 2005*). For additional programming insights see "Suicide Prevention Among Active Duty Air Force Personnel—United States, 1990-1999—summary of a suicide prevention program adopted by the U.S. Air Force." *Morbidity and Mortality Weekly Report,* Nov 26, 1999, viewed online on May 15, 2005. See also the Association for Student Judicial Affairs (ASJA) *Law and Policy Report,* Vols. 143 and 144 "Special Report: The Air Force Suicide Prevention Program," June 3 and 10, 2004. Additional information about the program can be found at: http://www.e-publishing.af.mil/pubfiles/af/44/afpam44-160/ afpam44-160.pdf (*Viewed May 15, 2005*), and in Appendix F.

118. See n. 117, *supra.* MIT has explicitly adopted several components of the Air Force program; see "MIT's mental health services featured on NBC's 'Today'" (October 22, 2004 MIT News release available at: http://web.mit.edu/newsoffice/2004/today.html (*Viewed May 15, 2005*).

119. Cited in the ASJA *Law and Policy Report,* Vol143 "Special Report: The Air Force Suicide Prevention Program," June 3, 2004.

120. Jean Twenge, "The age of anxiety? The birth cohort change in anxiety and neuroticism, 1952-1993." *Journal of Personality & Social Psychology.* 2000 Dec Vol 79(6) 1007-102.

121. See the suicide prevention training module for Resident Advisors in the appendix.

122. The power of the mentoring relationship was evident in one of Thomas Jefferson's reminisces about his education, published in Fawn Brodie's 1975 book: *Thomas Jefferson: An Intimate History* (Bantam), p. 27:

> I had the good fortune to become acquainted very early with some characters of very high standing, and to feel the incessant wish that I could even become what they were. Under temptations and difficulties I could ask myself what would Dr. Small, Mr. Wythe, Peyton Randolph do in this situation? What course in it will assure me their approbation? I am certain that this mode of deciding on my conduct tended more to its correctness than any reasoning power I possessed.

Jefferson met two of his three mentors (Small and Wythe) when he was a student at William and Mary. They were teachers who (in Fawn Brodie's words) "accepted him as one of them with affectionate admiration when he was only nineteen" (p. 63). Wythe in particular was described by Jefferson as "my second father... my ... earliest and best friend" (Brodie, p. 59). As friends, the impact of Jefferson's teachers went beyond the expansion of his "reasoning power" encompass character development through human connection. That influence was evident in 1818, when Jefferson wrote the founding "Report of the Commissioners for the University of Virginia" (The "Rockfish Gap Report). Among his comments about "[t]he best mode of government for youth, in large collections" was the observation that:

> The affectionate deportment between father and son, offers in truth the best example for that of tutor and pupil; and the experience and practice of other countries, in this respect, maybe worthy of enquiry and consideration with us.

(This note is adapted from a longer discussion of the topic in 02.26 *Synfax Weekly Report*, June 17, 2002, p. 3029).

123. "Faculty address mental health: Series educates professors, teachers on signs of mental health problems," University of Virginia *Cavalier Daily*, April 19, 2005. Viewed at http://www.cavalierdaily.com/CVArticle.asp?ID[5]23297&pid[5]1292 on May 15, 2005.

124. A good resource on this topic is Michael Bishop and J.D. Trout, *Epistemology and the Psychology of Human Judgment* (Oxford University Press, 2005).

125. Cited in the ASJA *Law and Policy Report*, Vol144 "Special Report: The Air Force Suicide Prevention Program, Part II" June 10, 2004.

126. The phenomenon of "lovesickness" (a possible precursor to depression and heightened suicide risk among college students) merits more attention from physicians and mental health professionals. See Frank Tallis "Crazy for you"*The Psychologist* Vol. 18 No.2 February 2005 P. 74:

> The average clinical psychologist will not receive referral letters from GPs and psychiatrists mentioning lovesickness; however, careful examination of the sanitized language will reveal that lovesickness may well be the underlying problem. Many people are referred for help who cannot cope with the intensity of love, have been destabilized by falling in love, or who suffer on account of their love being unrequited (a consequence of which might be attempted suicide, thus dramatizing the ancient contention that love can be fatal).

Morton M. Silverman, M.D. (A Distinguished Fellow of the American Psychiatric Association, Clinical Associate Professor of Psychiatry at the University of Chicago, and Senior Medical Advisor to the National Suicide Prevention Resource Center) reported at a December 1-2, 2005 American College Health Association Workshop that "[a]mong all 18-24 year olds who died by suicide . . . [a]lmost 50% were due to intimate partner problems." Dr. Silverman is co-author of a book we highly recommend: *Adolescent Suicide: Assessment and Intervention*, Second Edition by Alan Berman, David Jobes, and Martin Silverman, (American Psychological Association, 2005).

127. See Stovall and Domino, *supra*, n. 53. Among the questions they suggest are:
• Have you ever thought of killing yourself?
• How would you do it?
• What would happen to your family or significant others if you did that?
• What has kept you from acting on these thoughts?

128. See Ann H. Franke "Student Mental Health Screening: A Risk Management Perspective," at http://www.mentalhealthscreening.org/college/riskmanagement. htm (*viewed May 22, 2005*):

> Another element of the defense can be a record of prevention programs. Screening efforts and counseling services help show that the institution took student mental health issues seriously . . . When a tragedy does occur, they can also help in court. Consider screening programs as part of your institution's risk management efforts.

129. A good example is the group "Students for Mental Health Awareness" at the University of Virginia. See http://www.student.virginia.edu/mental/ (*viewed May 21 2005*). The group (in collaboration with University Counseling and Psychological Services) conducted an information and screening session reported in the March 25, 2005 *Cavalier Daily*. See: http://www.cavalierdaily.com/CVArticle.asp? ID[5]22877&pid[5]1276 (*Viewed May 22, 2005*).

130. Screening for Mental Health "Tips for Success" available at: http://www. mentalhealthscreening.org/college/tips.aspx (*Viewed May 22, 2005*)

131. *Supra*, n. 8.

132. "The Pressure Mounts," *US News & World Report,* April 11, 2005 p. 54-55

133. See http://www.jedfoundation.org/articles/UlifelineUpgrade.pdf (*viewed May 23, 2005*).

134. "Reaching out to students" *USA TODAY* online edition (posted December 6, 2004).

135. See "Worried Colleges Step Up Efforts Over Suicide" *New York Times,* December 3, 2004, p. 1:

> Cornell is making a special effort to reach out to Asian and Asian-American students. Of 16 students there who have committed suicide since 1996, 9 were of Asian descent. The university created a task force to explore those students' experience at Cornell and how to help them when they have problems, since they do not use Cornell's counseling services at the same rate as their classmates, said Susan H. Murphy, the university's vice president for student and academic services. Often when they do seek help, "they are in real crisis," Ms Murphy said.

136. See our expanded discussion of this topic in "Moving 'pre-beings' into the present," *Synfax Weekly Report* 04.10 week of March 15, 2004, p. 3233.

137. Carolyn Callahan, at the National Research Center on the Gifted and Talented at the University of Virginia, cited in "Perfect Problems: These Teens Are the Top in Everything, Including Stress," *Washington Post,* May 5, 2002, p. F1.

138. Few observers have described the current climate with greater clarity than former Czech Republic President Vaclav Havel: "Do you suppose," president Havel asked, there "might be a way to stop [the] blind perpetual motion dragging us into hell?" "Faith in the World," published in the April/May 1998 issue of *Civilization,* p. 53.

139. See "Hard-charging high schools urge students to do less," *The Christian Science Monitor,* March 21, 2005 online edition: http://www.csmonitor.com/2005/0321/p01s02-ussc.html (*viewed May 23, 2005*).

140. See, for example, readings and questions in the University of Maryland Academic Integrity Seminar: http://studentconduct.umd.edu/ethical/aca_integ.html (*viewed May 23, 2005*).

141. See "Marking a new era, Hopkins drops grades" ("A pass-fail system is replacing the traditional letters in doctors' education"). *Baltimore Sun* October 11, 2002 (online edition). Nearly half of the nation's top-ranked medical schools have shifted to some kind of pass/fail system. See the Eastern Michigan University *Echo Online* October 17, 2003 (viewed May 22, 2005): http://www.easternecho.com/cgi-bin/story.cgi?1130.

142. Competency based instructional models used by the armed forces are worthy of consideration. See, generally, the "competency coaching" approach used at the University of Pittsburgh Katz Graduate School of Business: http://www.katz.pitt.edu/cbcp.html (viewed May 23, 2005). A description of the model applied to undergraduate business and technical fields can be found at: http://www.stratford.edu/?page5competency (*viewed May 23, 2005*).

143. See, generally, Barbara Rubel (a consultant for the Department of Justice, Office for Victims of Crime), "The Grief Response Experienced by Survivors of Suicide" and extensive citations therein at http://www.griefworkcenter.com/newpage3.htm (*viewed May 23, 2005*).

144. This section draws upon the article "Suicide: the Aftermath" by Timothy Brooks in *Synfax Weekly Report* 01.47, November 12, 2001, p. 2057 and Robert Simon's

book *Assessing and Managing Suicide Risk: Guidelines for Clinically Based Risk Management* (American Psychiatric Publishing, 2004).

145. *Ibid* n. 143. American Association of Suicidology resources for survivors of suicide can be found at: http://www.suicidology.org/displaycommon.cfm?an=5 1&subarticlenbr=48 and at http://www.suicidology.org/displaycommon.cfm?an=14. (*Viewed May 29, 2005*). Guidance from the Canadian Association of Suicide Prevention (Healing . . . In the Aftermath of a Suicide") can be found at: http://www3. sympatico.ca/masecard/healing.html (*viewed on May 29, 2005*)

146. "And Still, Echoes of a Death Long Past," *The New York Times*, October 28, 2003 (citing research by David A. Brent, child and adolescent psychiatrist at the University of Pittsburgh) (*viewed May 29, 2005*).

147. Simon, *Ibid*, n. 38, p. 199. See also "Therapists as Survivors of Suicide: Basic Information" published by the American Association of Suicidology at: http://mypage.iusb.edu/ jmcintos/basicinfo.htm (*Viewed on May 29, 2005.*) See also "Patient Suicide Brings Therapists Lasting Pain" *New York Times*, January 16, 200. (*Viewed May 29, 2005*).

148. Simon, *Ibid*, n. 38, p. 204. Simon also suggests that "all entries made after the incident should be correctly dated," p. 206.

149. Simon, *Ibid*, n. 38, p. 198, 199. Simon (on p. 201) cited the American Psychiatric Association Guidelines on Confidentiality (1987):

Psychiatrists should remember that their ethical and legal responsibilities regarding confidentiality continue after their patients' deaths. In cases where the release of information would be injurious to the deceased patient's interests or reputation, care must be exercised to limit the released data to that which is necessary for the purpose stated in the [lawful] request for information.

But see the caveat in note 150, below.

150. Simon, *Ibid*, n. 38 provides a particularly helpful discussion of this topic on p. 207, including a candid statement that "maintenance of absolute confidentiality of the deceased patient [during conversations with family members] is usually not possible . . . To do so may defy common sense and may appear evasive."

151. Kay Redfield Jamison describes the "psychological autopsy" process in *Night Falls Fast* (*supra*, n. 13, p. 32):

Members of the [psychological autopsy] team interview friends, family members, and doctors of the victim, covering a comprehensive range of topics: [including] medical and psychiatric history . . . personality and lifestyle, . . . typical patterns of reaction to stress, [and] emotional upheavals . . .

From this information and a detailed analysis of the death itself, the . . . team puts together a description of the victim's last days and then presents its findings to the coroner or medical examiner. Often, in seemingly equivocal cases, the recommendation is a persuasive one for a verdict of suicide; in other instances, however, the evidence leads to a decision for accident . . .

152. See Ann Franke, *supra* n. 22.

153. Website of the American Foundation for Suicide Prevention: "Reporting on suicide: Recommendations for the media" (*viewed on May 28, 2005*) http://www. afsp.org/education/recommendations/1/index.html

See also the Centers for Disease Control (CDC) document "Suicide Contagion and the Reporting of Suicide: Recommendations from a National Workshop," (1994):

One risk factor that has emerged from this research is suicide "contagion," a process by which exposure to the suicide or suicidal behavior of one or more persons influences others to commit or attempt suicide. Evidence suggests that the effect of contagion is not confined to suicides occurring in discrete geographic areas ... [N]onfictional newspaper and television coverage of suicide has been associated with a statistically significant excess of suicides. The effect of contagion appears to be strongest among adolescents, and several well publicized "clusters" among young persons have occurred.

More recent findings from the Royal College of Psychiatrists (London) supports the CDC conclusion. See "Is suicide contagious? New study suggests imitative suicide occurs among mentally ill" (2004) available at: http://www.rcpsych. ac.uk/press/preleases/pr/pr_581.htm (*viewed May 27, 2005*).

See also Kay Redfield Jamison (*Supra*, n. 13, p. 276): "The contagious quality of suicide, or the tendency for suicide to occur in clusters, has been observed for centuries and is at least partially responsible for some of the ancient sanctions against the act of suicide."

154. Website of the American Foundation for Suicide Prevention: "Reporting on suicide: Recommendations for the media" (*viewed on May 28, 2005*): http://www. afsp.org/education/recommendations/5/index.html

155. See, e.g. Ann Franke's data (*supra*, n. 28) about the numbers of pending college student suicide liability lawsuits. The pendency of litigation, of course, does not mean that courts are ready to pronounce a new direction in the law.

156. A good example is the Richard Fossey and Perry Zirkel law review article, (*supra*, n. 34) on the limited precedential value of *Eisel v. Board of Education of Montgomery County* (*supra*, n. 31), holding that junior high school counselors had a duty to alert parents to suicidal statements attributed to the parent's child by fellow students.

157. See an article by University of Arizona Professor Barry Goldman and EEOC administrator Edward McCaffrey in the Winter 1999 issue of *Synthesis: Law and Policy in Higher Education* ("Why Fair Treatment Matters," p. 738). Research they reviewed indicated that individuals were less likely to litigate adverse decisions if they believed those decisions were grounded in a fair procedure (allowing different views to be heard), and explained with courtesy. See also our discussion of the Phillips Academy case, *supra* n. 92 and *Thomas v. Davidson Academy*, *supra*, n. 102.

158. See n. 116, *supra* on the success of the University of Illinois program in keeping students in school, "following even a serious suicide attempt."

159. A thoughtful review of two articles in the *American Medical News* about "The Role of Forgiveness in Medicine" can be found at: http://www.mercola.com/2000/ sep/3/forgiveness.htm (*Last viewed May 30, 2005*).

The authors reported that:

One study found almost a quarter of suits were prompted by patients' realization that physicians had failed to be completely honest or had intentionally misled them when a mishap occurred. More than a third of British patients participating in another study said they wouldn't have sued if they'd been offered a full explanation and apology ... Even if a suit can't be prevented, apologies can reduce animosity enough to speed a settlement, maintains Dr. Jonathan R. Cohen, PhD, an expert on negotiation, dispute resolution and evidence at the University of Florida's law school. Dr Cohen also stated that "[w]here people can freely admit their errors and take responsibility for them, the organization becomes better at preventing errors."

Appendices

Appendix A

Student Suicide: A Case Study
The Story of "WR"

The student "WR" committed suicide years ago. This case study was prepared at the time by a college administrator who tried to understand the circumstances. WR's family provided assistance and authorized publication. This is not a "composite" or a fictional account.

In the draft of a personal letter found in his desk, "WR" wrote "I want to give of myself." In that spirit, we hope his thoughts, experiences, and feelings will help others understand some of the fears and emotions of college life, and the need to offer professional assistance, and friendship.

Commentary from the text of this monograph is provided so the case study can be used as an independent resource for staff training.

Circumstances prior to WR's suicide

WR was a 19-year old engineering student at a large, competitive, public university in the Midwest. He committed suicide on an early May afternoon by jumping without warning from the tenth floor of his residence hall room.

WR's suicide appears to have been related to his involvement in an automobile accident approximately thirty minutes before his death. WR was ticketed for following too closely. The other driver suffered a minor whiplash injury, and was visibly "in pain and nervous" while being prepared for transport to the hospital. Damage was done to the front of the car WR was driving. That car belonged to his sister; WR's mother had told him not to drive it.

WR was in the midst of fraternity initiation when he died. A class-mate saw him falling asleep in class, and heard him state he had little sleep in "the past two weeks." WR was also under academic pressure and falling behind in laboratory projects. He spent much of the day of his death attempting to complete a chemistry assignment.

WR's suicide does not seem to have been planned in advance. On the evening before (or morning of) his death he prepared a schedule that listed activities well into the evening. Nonetheless, WR had given thought to suicide. He was writing a psychology paper on the suicide of a childhood friend. His writing was clinical and analytical, but most characteristics of his friend matched his own.

Personality Characteristics

Friends and family members stated WR was a good student (B+ average in a demanding program) with a high achievement orienta-tion. Winning for him was a passion. Losing led to uncontrollable out-bursts of emotion directed toward himself. He viewed college life as a series of "challenges" leading (hopefully) to "victories."

WR frequently displayed a negative self-image and was troubled by a stuttering problem. Occasionally he was perceptive enough to see some of his seeming shortcomings as illusory. On other occasions he was overcome by depression and anxiety.

Outwardly WR seemed untroubled, but was described by acquain-tances as "lonely." He mentioned to a classmate that he was not well accepted by other residents on his residence hall floor. Later, WR told the same classmate that he was not a good fit with the fraternity he had joined.

WR expressed interest in being a teacher or a lawyer, but felt his stuttering problem precluded either choice. He enjoyed the fine arts, and was a good artist, but felt chemical engineering was a more cer-tain path to success.

Comments in WR's Notes and Papers

WR was withdrawn and reticent. Perhaps for those reasons he chose to record many of his deepest thoughts and fears on the mar-gins of his school notebooks. Comments expressing fear and anxiety are often related to academic work on the remainder of the page. Other jottings were found on his desk and in drafts of letters and themes. WR's need to express himself in writing (often in dated formats) pro-vides an extraordinary insight into his feelings and college experien-ces. They are feelings and experiences other students may be having now, even as they appear outwardly untroubled.

WR's comments are placed in order of recurring general themes. For example, he commented most frequently on what might be termed

"achievement orientation/ grades/ selfconfidence," and that group-
ing appears first below. Within particular groupings comments are
placed in chronological order whenever possible.

Achievement orientation / grades / self confidence

[1] *Carved on his residence hall desk:* "I can" (Time unknown).

[2] *Chemistry notebook:* "The feeling in my stomach October 14, is one
of turning, grinding. I can't feel more sorry for myself. Yet I want to
blame my failures on others. I refuse to accept the fault as mine. I hope
I'll turn to hate the other members of my class, to punish them and
myself, and to come out of this. Today I felt like quitting. Tonight I'll
fight on reinforced ground and I need confidence in a victory" (October 14).

[3] *Chemistry notebook:* "I'm scared" (October 18-19).

[4] *Chemistry notebook:* "Help, I'm scared. Oh, I'm scared! I don't want
to lose (late first semester).

[5] *Cover of returned chemistry examination:* "Would it be worth my effort to attempt scrounging 2 points from No. 2 on Section II?" (December, close of first semester).

[6] *Draft of personal letter:* "My Chem. exam which I thought I pulled
a *D* on and got tremendously shook and vowed to become an artist
or join the army or live in the mountains ... turned out to be a high
B" (middle second semester).

[7] *Notes on his desk:* "Afraid to talk in class ... Must impress others.
Need to prove myself" (late second semester).

[8] *Notes on his desk:* "Fear!! Put there by yourself ... You can't do it?
(late second semester).

[9] *Draft of personal letter:* "I want to give of myself" (late second semester).

[10] *Mathematics notebook:* "Don't stagnate, go forward, improve" (April
28).

[11] *Selection from his psychology paper on suicide:* [the suicide victim]
"felt a need to prove himself and exerted total effort" (early May).

[12] *Selection from his psychology paper on suicide:* "The competition for
high school esteem in academics, sports, or social circles is stiff and
develops sturdy, healthy Americans" (early May).

[13] *Selection from his psychology paper on suicide:* "Reality confronts the
'bottom people.' They often quit school, join the army, or find a job.
Admitting the plight of being unable to handle the school system's

competition requires courage; and parental or administrative psychological guidance should be available to help recognize the problem" (early May).

Stutter

[1] *Chemistry notebook:* "Can I ever teach? Will I ever cure stuttering? Job interviews, phone calls. People notice or am I blowing this out of proportion?" (Early second semester).

[2] *Psychology notebook:* "When I talk it's always bad. So I hide away" (Early second semester).

[3] *Selection from rough draft of unidentified theme:* "Being unable to express yourself parallels the tyranny of a dictator" (Second semester).

[4] *Selection from rough draft of unidentified theme:* "After my father ordered me to stop talking spastic I felt ashamed and guilty to stutter" (Second semester).

[5] *Selection from rough draft of unidentified theme:* "[Stuttering] is no joke ... self-consciousness or inferiority complexes often result from the stammerer's ventures in life. Stutterers shy away from a job as a T. A., or eliminate the fields of teaching or law" (Second semester).

[6] *Psychology notebook:* "[I] and [R] [siblings] talked fast. Start fresh now" (Second semester).

[7] *Paper on top of his residence hall desk:* "Sitting in class the other day, alone, I realized I could say anything I want. In the presence of others I block myself, I hold myself back" (late second semester).

[8] *Chemistry notebook:* "A way to communicate, if I stutter I lower myself" (March 31).

Loneliness

[1] *Scrap of paper in his top desk drawer:* "I am alone and bored" (new student week).

[2] *Spanish notebook:* "Don't get disillusioned, talk to no one" (early first semester).

[3] *Psychology workbook:* "Don't trust people" (early second semester).

[4] *Psychology workbook:* "Do things on your own" (early second semester).

[5] *Mathematics notebook:* "[Classroom observation] everyone reacts cold at first, eyes upraised, teacher never smiles" (February 8).

[6] *Mathematics notebook:* "RR [student name and telephone number]. Mr. RR would you please call?" (February 18).

[7] *Mathematics notebook:* "I need, need, need" (March 18).

[8] *Selection from his psychology paper on suicide:* "His [the victim's] strong pride hindered him from sharing his problems with others and being an involuntary loner increased his frustration" (early May).

Depression
[1] *Sketch pad:* "depression" (written next to sketched figure of boy with head bowed) (date unknown).

[2] *Mathematics notebook:* "depressed, oh depressed. Love-equal relationship" (early April).

[3] *Paper on his desk:* "Problem exists. Worried, upset, eating a lot, depressed" (late second semester).

[4] *Rough draft of personal letter:* "If the right people approach me presently I may turn God-squad" (late second semester).

[5] *Mathematics notebook:* "A learned response got me down" (late April).

[6] *Envelope among papers on his desk:* "World ugly face facts kill coward" (late second semester, perhaps early May).

Guilt
[1] *Carved on his residence hall desk:* "You're selfish" (time unknown).

[2] *Freshman English notebook:* "In my room guilt. Family did not accept" (October).

[3] *Mathematics notebook:* "Guilty, Guilty (February)

[4] *Rough draft of personal letter:* "I still get selfish moods, but now I try to catch myself" (late second semester).

[5] *Among papers on his desk:* "You're shook over nothing. You did nothing and you're ready to jump up in arms" (late second semester).

Aggression / Anger
[1] *High school math-science notebook (in college residence hall room):* "Hate" (early senior year of high school).

[2] *Psychology notebook:* "Kill" (February).

[3] *Rough draft of unidentified theme in physics notebook; account of childhood fight with a girl on the block. After losing the fight:* "my family and friends' laughs went on seemingly for hours, a tension mounted inside me. I had to kill Suzy. I was angry and bitter. Suddenly I punched her right in the nose. I hit her again and knocked her down. I wasn't satisfied, I wanted to kill her. Then she started to cry. I stopped. I felt like I had just beat my mother (time unknown).

[4] *Selection from his psychology paper on suicide:* "Occasional violent flashes of temper were [the suicide victim's] uncontrollable emotions representing his true feeling" (early May).

Note: *Acquaintances spoke of occasions when WR lost friendly wrestling matches and broke into tears or uncontrollable anger.*

Compilation of interview comments from family members; residence staff members; and other residents:

"He loved Hitler and read all those books on him."

"Concerned about people, frequently sad, asked how anyone could be happy while others are in wheel chairs."

"Wrestling with friend at home, friend too large, WR grew frustrated, hit with fist while issuing cries."

"Always had terrible temper."

"Stuttering bothered him.'

"Bothered him an awful lot that he never did as well as he thought he could."

"Stayed with the fraternity only because of the challenge."

"Was against suicide as he felt no one had the right to give up."

"Felt inferior."

"Extremely poor loser."

"Got on well with father and mother."

"Always nervous about damage to car."

"Always set schedule for himself; said that by sixteen should be going with girls."

"Always down."

"Hated speech therapy class group system."

"Never let on when depressed."

"Really proud."

"Felt chemistry teachers were out to get him."

"Did not seem like he ever talked to anyone."

COMMENTARY

[1] **A definitive book on suicide is Kay Redfield Jamison's** *Night Falls Fast* (Knopf, 1999). She wrote that "the overwhelming majority of suicides are linked to psychiatric illnesses, so it is not surprising that many

of the notes and records left behind reflect the misery, cumulative despair, and hopelessness of those conditions" (p. 81). Jamison advised that "[i]f a family member or friend is acutely suicidal, it may be necessary to take away their credit cards, car keys, and checkbooks and to be supportive but firm in getting them to an emergency room or walk-in clinic. If a person is violent it may be necessary to call the police . . . These are difficult things to do but often essential" (p. 259).

If one thing can be learned from recent cases involving possible professional and institutional liability for student suicide it is that colleges may be too reluctant (and too slow) in hospitalizing students at risk of suicide. Consider this observation from a Massachusetts Superior Court in *Shin v. MIT* (2005):

> The Plaintiffs' argue that MIT medical professionals individually and collectively failed to coordinate Elizabeth's care. As a "treatment team" the professionals failed to secure Elizabeth's short term safety in response to Elizabeth's suicide plan in the morning hours of April 10. During the "deans and psychs" meeting on the morning of April 10, plans to assist Elizabeth were discussed, however, an immediate response to Elizabeth's escalating threats to commit suicide were not formulated. By not formulating and enacting an immediate plan to respond to Elizabeth's escalating threats to commit suicide, the plaintiffs have put forth sufficient evidence of a genuine issue of material fact as to whether the MIT medical professionals were grossly negligent in their treatment of Elizabeth (p.16).

Hospitalization should not be undertaken primarily as a risk management strategy, but neither should it be rejected due to fear of embarrassment, inconvenience, or "One Flew Over the Cuckoo's Nest" stereotypes. A powerful insight in this regard can be found in William Styron's book *Darkness Visible* (a story of his battle with clinical depression). Reflecting upon his depression, his preparations to commit suicide, and the timely intervention of his wife (who arranged admission to a hospital) Styron wrote that:

> Many psychiatrists, who simply do not seem to be able to comprehend the nature and depth of the anguish their patients are undergoing, maintain their stubborn allegiance to pharmaceuticals in the belief that eventually the pills will kick in, the patient will respond, and the somber surroundings of the hospital will be avoided . . . [I]n fact, the hospital was my salvation, and it is something of a paradox that in this austere place with its locked and wired doors and desolate green hallways—ambulances screeching night and day ten floors below—I found the repose, the assuagement of the tempest in my brain, that I was unable to find in my [home] . . . [T]he hospital. . .offers the mild, oddly gratifying trauma of sudden stabilization . . . into an orderly and benign detention where one's only duty is to get well (pp. 68-69).

[2] **Jamison and others stress the importance of not romanticizing youth suicide.** It reflects a disturbed and tormented life, not an artistic temperament longing for a Platonic realm. Youth suicide is a horrible and wasteful failure, inflicting permanent suffering on the survivors. There is no nobility in it.

[3] **Suicide is unpredictable,** especially when individuals like WR are determined to hide their distress from others. His comments "[d]on't get disillusioned, talk to no one" and "don't trust people" reflected a failed strategy to draw on an inner strength he didn't possess. He persisted in his self-imposed separation, even as he recognized the limitations of that approach (blaming a friend's suicide on "strong pride," that "hindered him from sharing his problems with others"). In short, although WR gave warning signs of suicide, he kept virtually all of them to himself. There is no record he made a prior suicide attempt—the most reliable predictor of suicide.

What stands out about WR is his loneliness. That should attract the attention of gatekeepers (like residence advisors), not simply as a means to prevent suicide, but as a stimulus to build stronger communities. Colleges that develop vibrant communities; help students find challenges beyond a focus on the self; promote alternatives to substance abuse; and encourage character development (with the related capacity for impulse control) are already engaging in serious suicide prevention efforts.

[4] **Suicide can be a window on the nature and quality of learning.** Do most faculty members know—really *know*—that students have an inner life, and are astute observers? Consider WR's cryptic classroom comment, recorded in the margins of his mathematics notebook: "everyone reacts cold at first, eyes upraised, teacher never smiles." Teachers and college administrators should know that the richest forms of learning and development occur in the realm of the *personal*—mutual respect, affection, playfulness, guidance, and encouragement, including setting and rewarding high standards for performance. Students are hungry for this kind of personal contact, but are less likely to find it as higher education rushes into the digital world. The loss of the personal may not be evident in objective scales of acquired "knowledge," but can be seen in wounds to the soul, measured by exploding rates of depression and alcohol abuse.

[5] **Creative ways need to be found to encourage troubled students to see therapists.** Some students simply need reassurance. Others require treatment, or emergency intervention. The key is to create a climate where talking about personal problems with a mental health professional isn't stigmatized as some sort of failure. Outreach is essential, especially where students live. Holding a program on sui-

cide prevention, of course, may not attract the right audience. What is more likely to work is a broader approach, starting with topics students find more inviting—like forming and maintaining relationships, becoming effective leaders, or promoting health and fitness. Worked into each program should be thoughtful (sometimes subliminal) messages: people are complex; they benefit from self-insight; self-insight is gained not only in turning inward, but in reaching out to others; mental health professional have special skills and training in that regard; they can help.

[6] **Persistent loneliness, violent outbursts, or a sudden retreat into isolation, are indications of depression, or other forms of mental illness.** It's when those kinds of behaviors occur that gatekeepers need professional support. Ideally, that support will be woven into existing structures, like established liaison with counselors assigned to particular living units.

In serious cases, an ongoing "team" approach works best, involving multiple skills and responsibilities, including professional suicide assessment risk, law enforcement, legal counsel, and academic/administrative management, including contact with parents. In all but the most extraordinary circumstances, it should be presumed (consistent with the legal requirements of medical privilege) that parents or guardians are essential parts of any team trying to assist their offspring.

[7] **The causes of suicide are often complex.** Just as it is wrong to see suicide solely as an expression of existential anguish, it's premature to claim suicide can be understood and treated exclusively from traditional medical or psychological perspectives, especially quick, single-minded reliance upon pharmaceutical responses. Jamison (supra) wrote in this regard that "the threshold of suicidal behavior can be raised (that is, suicide can, to a limited extent, be protected against) by religious beliefs . . . [and] strong social supports" (p. 199). Such supports, Jamison believes may have "limited value" to individuals already predisposed to suicide, but they could be critical to minimizing or redirecting the accumulated psychic injuries that promote depression, and many other mental disorders.

Mental health professionals are also finding that various forms of "Cognitive-Behavior Therapy" (CBT) (systematic examination of underlying beliefs and behaviors), sometimes in combination with anti-depressant or anti-psychotic drugs, help produce sustained improvement, even in cases of serious mental illness (see, e.g. "Cognitive-Behavior Therapy for Treating Patients with Schizophrenia," April 2000, *Journal Watch Psychiatry*, p. 30). In the case of WR, for example, there were times when his mind was struggling for self-insight, endeavoring to heal itself (e.g. '[w]ill I ever cure stuttering? Job interviews, phone calls. People notice or am I blowing this out of proportion?"). From this broader perspective, educators (to borrow Plato's phrase) can be "physicians of the soul," helping students learn how to think carefully and deeply.

Appendix B

OCR Letter Rulings
Suicide Threats / Attempts & the ADA

BLUFFTON UNIVERSITY

Administrators must not take counsel of their legal fears and routinely dismiss students at risk of suicide. Not only would such a practice be ethically and educationally indefensible (e.g. students sent home often have ready access to firearms, the most frequent method of suicide), it might also violate the Americans with Disabilities Act, thereby engendering more litigation. Letter rulings issued by the Office of Civil Rights (OCR) of the U.S. Department of Education help clarify this point. A December 22, 2004 letter to the President of Bluffton University follows. Italicized sections reflect requirements that may be frequently overlooked by college administrators.

[Full text OCR Letter ruling; emphasis added]

Dr. Lee Snyder
President
Bluffton University
1 University Drive
Bluffton, Ohio 45817-2104

Re: OCR Complaint #15-04-2042

Dear Dr. Snyder:

This letter is to advise you of the disposition of the above-referenced complaint, which was received by the U.S. Department of Education, Office for Civil Rights (OCR), on July 2, 2004. The complaint alleged that Bluffton University (formerly known as Bluffton College) excluded a student from participation in its academic program on the basis of disability. Specifically, the complaint alleged that the University demanded that the Student either withdraw immediately or be indefinitely suspended after her attempted suicide in spring of 2004, and refused to reconsider this decision subsequent to receiving information about the Student's disability (bipolar disorder).

OCR is responsible for enforcing Section 504 of the Rehabilitation Act of 1973, 29 U.S.C. §794, and its implementing regulation at 34 C.F.R. Part 104. Section 504 prohibits discrimination based on disability by recipients of Federal financial assistance from the U.S. Department of Education. The University is a recipient of Federal financial assistance from the Department. OCR, therefore, has jurisdiction over this complaint.

In making a determination on this complaint, OCR interviewed the Complainant, the Student, the Student's mother, and the University official with direct knowledge of the case. In addition, OCR reviewed documentation provided by the Complainant and the University related to the allegation. Based on a careful analysis of this information, OCR determined that the University's actions in this situation did not comply with the requirements of the Section 504 regulation. However, the University has agreed to take action to resolve the compliance issues raised during this investigation. The basis for OCR's determination is discussed below.

Background and Findings of Fact

The Student entered the University as a freshman at the end of August 2003. In the spring of 2004, while in her dormitory room, the Student cut herself and took an overdose of pills in an apparent suicide attempt. The Student was hospitalized for approximately one week, during which time she was diagnosed for the first time with bipolar disorder. During her hospitalization she worked with mental health professionals who agreed that it would be beneficial to the Student to return to her studies upon her discharge.

Three days after the Student's suicide attempt, a University official (Official) spoke with the Student's mother and told her that the Student was being immediately withdrawn from the University. The Official told OCR that, in consultation with you, he made this decision based on the serious nature of the incident. In a letter to the Student dated five days after the suicide attempt, the Official stated that, "because of the behavior [the Student] exhibited," she was expected to immediately withdraw from the University and would be permitted on campus only to pick up her belongings. The letter stated that if the Student did not withdraw, the University would have no choice but to suspend her. The letter stated that it was in her best interest and that of the University that she leave the University and "receive the kind of professional help" not available at the school. Finally, the letter stated that if the Student wanted to return to the University, she would have to apply for readmission and submit information provided by "the appropriate counselors and/or doctors that [she is] fully capable of functioning as a student." In closing the letter, the Official again encouraged the Student to seek professional help. The Official did not contact any of the Student's treating physicians or counselors before sending this letter, nor did he contact the Student. He also did not review any of the Student's medical or counseling records in making this decision.

OCR's investigation revealed that the Student did not consent to the withdrawal and did not submit or sign any forms or statements suggesting her intent to withdraw from the University. There were no withdrawal papers in her student file. The only record the University could produce regarding the Student's withdrawal was an email from the Official to employees in the Registrar's office stating that the Student had been withdrawn from the University effective the date of his letter to the Student.

Approximately one week after the Official sent the withdrawal letter to the Student, the Student's mental health counselor, a licensed social worker, sent a letter to the Official that stated that the Student was now able to cope with her mental illness and that she was no longer suicidal. The letter discussed the treatment anticipated for the Student and informed the University that the counselor had encouraged the Student to resume her studies and get back to her routine. The University made no attempt to contact the counselor after receipt of that letter and did not rescind its decision to withdraw the Student. The counselor also telephoned the Official shortly after her letter to discuss the Student's condition and anticipated treatment and to ask him to reconsider his decision. The Official told OCR that he refused to reconsider the decision and that he could not recall whether he had explained to the counselor what type of documentation the Student would need to submit to be able to return to the University. The Official stated to OCR that he was concerned that the Student would attempt suicide again.

That same week, the Student and her mother met with the Official and requested permission for the Student to return to the University immediately to finish the semester, which request the Official denied. The Official told OCR that, should the Student reapply to the University in the future, she would have to submit documentation from a medical professional indicating a diagnosis, treatment plan, and prognosis. He told OCR that he did not accept the information that the Student's mental health counselor, the Student, and her mother had provided but could not recall whether he explained to the Student or her mother what information would be sufficient or necessary for her to return.

Following this meeting, the Complainant wrote several letters to the Official on the Student's behalf wherein she asserted that the University's actions in involuntarily withdrawing the Student constituted disability discrimination. The University's response to the first letter was a one-paragraph letter stating that the Student's withdrawal was considered to be an emergency withdrawal and that she received a full refund of her tuition for the semester. The University responded to a second letter from the Complainant by following up on the tuition refund and thanking the Complainant for sending information on the law concerning direct threat. OCR found that the University neither took any action to address the Complainant's allegations that the actions taken by the University regarding the Student were discriminatory nor to advise the Complainant how to file a formal grievance. OCR's review of the University's Student Handbook revealed that it does not identify, by name or title, a responsible employee to coordinate its efforts to comply with Section 504 regulations and does not set forth any grievance procedures providing for the prompt and equitable resolution of disability discrimination complaints. The Official confirmed that the University has no specific grievance procedures for Section 504 complaints.

There is no provision in the Student Handbook, or in any of the documentation the University provided to OCR, that defines, describes, or mentions an emergency withdrawal or related procedures. The Student Handbook does set forth a judicial process for when a person is accused of violating an academic standard or violating the Honor System, giving students the right to a 72-hour notice of a charge and hearing and, if necessary, an appeal. However, the University did not give the Student the opportunity to use this process to appeal her withdrawal.

The Official could not recall for OCR any other instance where a student was required to withdraw from the University. Records the University provided for the 2002-2003 and 2003-2004 academic years show that there were no emergency withdrawals or involuntary withdrawals for the 2002-2003 or 2003-2004 academic years. The Official did recall that a student who was seriously physically injured in an accident was once withdrawn from the University by her parent. This student was not required by the University to submit medical records, a treatment plan, or a prognosis upon her return. The Official could recall only one other instance where the University imposed the same requirements for return that were made for the Student's return. In that case, a student working at the University over the summer of 2003 began to exhibit what the Official deemed to be symptoms of mental illness and was asked to leave. That student was not allowed to return until he provided the University with documentation showing a diagnosis, a treatment plan, and a prognosis.

In addition, during the course of this investigation, OCR found that the University's policy concerning requests for modifications and accommodations for students with disabilities only applies on its face to students with learning disabilities. The Faculty Handbook does provide a more general definition of eligibility for disability services, but this is not distributed to students at the University. The policy found in the Student Handbook also does not specify the documentation that must be submitted to provide notice of a disability, nor to whom it must be submitted or when.

Applicable Regulatory Standards

Pursuant to the Section 504 implementing regulation, at 34 C.F.R. §104.3(j)(1), an individual with a disability is any person who has a physical or mental impairment which substantially limits one or more major life activities, has a record of such an impairment, or is regarded as having such an impairment. Under 34 C.F.R. §104.3(j)(2)(i)(b), a physical or mental impairment includes any mental or psychological disorder, such as mental illness. Under 34 C.F.R. §104.3(l)(3), a qualified individual with a disability, with respect to post-secondary education, is one who meets the academic and technical standards requisite to participation in the recipient's education program. 34 C.F.R. §104.3(j)(2)(iv) states that a person regarded as having a disability is a person who does not have a physical or mental impairment that substantially limits a major life activity but who is treated by others as having such a limitation. Further, pursuant to 34 C.F.R. §104.43, no qualified student with a disability shall, on the basis of disability, be excluded from participation in, be denied the benefits of, or otherwise be subjected to discrimination under any postsecondary education program or activity.

OCR policy holds that nothing in Section 504 prevents educational institutions from addressing the dangers posed by an individual who represents a "direct threat" to the health and safety of self or others, even if such an individual is a person with a disability, as that individual may no longer be qualified for a particular educational program or activity. *However, recipients must take steps to ensure that disciplinary and other adverse actions against persons posing a direct threat are not a pretext or excuse for discrimination.*

To rise to the level of a direct threat, there must be a high probability of substantial harm and not just a slightly increased, speculative, or remote risk. In a direct threat situation, a college needs to make an individualized and objective assessment of the student's ability to safely participate in the college's program, based on a reasonable medical judgment relying on the most current medical knowledge or the best available objective evidence. The assessment must determine: the nature, duration, and severity of the risk; the probability that the potentially threatening injury will actually occur;

and whether reasonable modifications of policies, practices, or procedures will sufficiently mitigate the risk. Due process requires a college to adhere to procedures to ensure that students with disabilities are not subject to adverse action on the basis of unfounded fear, prejudice, or stereotypes. A nondiscriminatory belief will be based on a student's observed conduct, actions, and statements, not merely knowledge or belief that the student is an individual with a disability. In exceptional circumstances, such as situations where safety is of immediate concern, a college may take interim steps pending a final decision regarding adverse action against a student as long as minimal due process (such as notice and an initial opportunity to address the evidence) is provided in the interim and full due process (including a hearing and the right to appeal) is offered later.

Finally, the Section 504 regulation at 34 C.F.R. §104.7 requires recipients with fifteen or more employees to designate a responsible employee to coordinate Section 504 compliance efforts *and to adopt grievance procedures that incorporate appropriate due process standards and that provide for the prompt and equitable resolution of Section 504 complaints.* The regulation, at 34 C.F.R. §104.44(a), also requires postsecondary institutions to make such modifications to its academic requirements as are necessary to ensure that such requirements do not discriminate or have the effect of discriminating, on the basis of disability, against a qualified student with a disability.

Analysis

The Student was admitted to the University and, therefore, is qualified within the meaning of Section 504. The evidence supports that, although the Student had not been diagnosed as having bipolar disorder at the time she was involuntarily withdrawn, the University regarded her as having a mental disability that was substantially limiting. *The University withdrew the Student following her suicide attempt because of its perception that she was mentally ill and incapable of functioning as a student,* as evidenced by the letter the Official sent to the Student and OCR's interview of the Official concerning his decision. *The University required the Student to submit evidence from a medical professional of her diagnosis, a treatment plan, and her prognosis before she would be eligible to reapply. This requirement has only been imposed on one other student at the University, a student who the same Official also regarded as mentally ill.* Moreover, when the Student was seeking to return to the University, she advised the University that she was diagnosed as having bipolar disorder, and the University does not dispute that the Student has a disability. Thus, OCR finds that the Student is a qualified individual with a disability under Section 504.

In withdrawing the Student from the University, the University did not afford the Student due process. Despite being notified of the Student's disability and receiving documentation and information concerning her ability to return to school from the counselor, the Student, and the Student's mother, the Official refused to reconsider the withdrawal decision. The Official could not recall whether he explained to the Student and her mother the documentation required for the Student to return. The evidence shows that the Official failed to consider the information about the Student's condition that was presented, did not explain what was insufficient about the submitted information to the Student and her mother, and would not allow the Student to return to school that semester.

The University did not specifically state that the Student posed a direct threat to herself or others as its reason for withdrawing the Student. OCR examined this possible defense, however, because the University stated that the Student was removed because of a fear that she would attempt suicide again. OCR found that the evidence does not support a defense based on direct threat. The University did not consult with medical personnel, examine objective evidence, ascertain the nature, duration and severity of the risk to the Student or other students, or consider mitigating the risk of injury to the Student or other students. The University made the decision without providing the Student notice of a hearing or an opportunity to be heard. Rather, the evidence showed that the University made a determination to withdraw the Student within forty-eight hours of her attempted suicide based on a conversation between the Official and you.

Finally, the University does not have any formal Section 504 grievance procedures addressing Section 504 grievances and, therefore, did not address the Complainant's disability discrimination allegations against the University. The University's policies also do not designate a specific Section 504 Coordinator as required by Section 504. In addition, the University's limited policies on students with disabilities only include learning disabilities and do not provide information for a student to be able to determine how to notify the University of a disability or need for academic adjustments or auxiliary aids and services.

Commitment to Resolve

On December 15, 2004, the University agreed to implement the enclosed agreement to resolve the compliance issues identified during our investigation. Pursuant to the agreement, the University will: reimburse the Student for any room fees and books for spring semester 2004 that have not already been returned to her; develop a written policy establishing reasonable emergency removal and return conditions consistent with the direct threat standards explained above; develop policies and procedures that comply with Section 504 for the participation of students with disabilities in the University's programs and for the provision of necessary academic adjustments and auxiliary aids and services to students with disabilities; and develop grievance procedures that incorporate appropriate due process standards and that provide for the prompt and equitable resolution of complaints alleging disability discrimination. OCR will monitor the implementation of the agreement.

Based on the above, we are closing this complaint as of the date of this letter. OCR appreciates the courtesy and cooperation shown by your staff and counsel during the investigation and resolution of this complaint. We look forward to receiving your first monitoring report, which is due February 7, 2005. If you have any questions or concerns about the resolution of this complaint, please contact Ms. Ann Millette . . .

Sincerely,

Rhonda Bowman
Team Leader, Cleveland Office
Midwestern Division

COMMITMENT TO RESOLVE
Bluffton University
OCR Complaint –15-04-2042

Bluffton University (the University) submits to the U.S. Department of Education, Office for Civil Rights (OCR), this Commitment to Resolve to resolve the allegations in the above-referenced complaint, and to ensure compliance with Section 504 of the Rehabilitation Act of 1973, (Section 504) 29 U.S.C. §794, and its implementing regulation at 34 C.F.R. Part 104. In entering into this Commitment to Resolve, the University makes no admission that it has violated Section 504.

REMEDIAL PROVISIONS
A.   By January 31, 2005, the University will reimburse the Student for the amount of her room fees that have not yet been returned and for the cost of her course books for spring semester 2004, when she was involuntarily withdrawn by the University.

B.   By January 31, 2005, the University will designate a responsible employee to serve as its coordinator for Section 504 compliance in accordance with 34 C.F.R. §104.7(a) and will publish the name or title and contact information for that employee, on a continuing basis, in its recruitment materials and general publications, including the Student Handbook, in accordance with 34 C.F.R. §104.8.

C.   By March 7, 2005, the University will develop a written policy that establishes reasonable emergency removal and return conditions, consistent with direct threat standards, for students with mental or psychological conditions who are placed on administrative leave or involuntary withdrawal for medical reasons or who request a voluntary withdrawal or leave of absence. The policy will indicate that the University's Section 504 Coordinator and other appropriate persons knowledgeable about the student's condition will be involved where students are removed or seek a return to the University pursuant to this policy.

D.   By March 7, 2005, the University will develop policies and procedures that comply with the requirements of the Section 504 implementing regulation at 34 C.F.R. §§104.43-104.44 for the participation of students with disabilities in the University's programs and for the provision of necessary academic adjustments and auxiliary aids and services to students with disabilities, including students who have disabilities other than learning disabilities, such as psychiatric disabilities. The University's policies and procedures will identify specifically what reasonable steps students with disabilities must take to notify the University of their disability and their need for academic adjustments or auxiliary aids and services.

E.   By March 7, 2005, the University will, in accordance with the Section 504 implementing regulation at 34 C.F.R. §104.7(b), develop grievance procedures that incorporate appropriate due process standards and that provide for the prompt and equitable resolution of complaints alleging discrimination based upon disability.

F.   By May 20, 2005, and after notification from OCR that the policies and procedures developed in accordance with paragraphs C-E above are consistent with the requirements of Section 504, the University will notify students, faculty, and staff of the new policies and procedures by posting them on the University's website, including them in the Student Handbook, and other effective means of notification.

G.   By May 20, 2005, the University will provide training from an individual who is knowledgeable about Section 504 to its designated Section 504 coordinator regarding the University's obligations to students with disabilities under Section 504 and its implementing regulation, including but not necessarily limited to the provision of necessary academic adjustments and related aids and services, the requirement that the University's recruitment materials and publications contain a notice of nondiscrimination under Section 504 and contact information for the 504 Coordinator, the prohibition against preadmission inquiries into disability (e.g., asking teachers about a student's "emotional stability"), the direct threat standards, and the requirement to have a prompt and equitable grievance procedure for disability discrimination complaints.

REPORTING REQUIREMENTS

1. By February 7, 2005, the University will submit to OCR documentation verifying its implementation of paragraphs A-B above, a copy of the reimbursement check issued by the University to the Student, identification of the name, title, and contact information for the University's designated Section 504 coordinator, and copies of the notifications issued regarding the University's Section 504 coordinator.

2. By March 14, 2005, the University will submit to OCR for review copies of the policies and procedures developed pursuant to paragraphs C-E above.

3. By May 31, 2005, the University will submit to OCR documentation verifying its implementation of paragraphs F-G above, including a copy of the notifications to faculty, staff, and students regarding its new policies and procedures, the date of the training, the name and qualifications of the trainer, and a copy of the training agenda and any training materials.

MARIETTA COLLEGE

The abridged text of a July 26, 2005 OCR letter (Midwestern Division) to Dr. Jean Scott, President of Marietta College follows. We have italicized requirements we think are frequently overlooked by college administrators.

Dear Dr. Scott:

This letter is to advise you of the disposition of ... [a] complaint, which was received by the U.S. Department of Education, Office for Civil Rights (OCR), on September 20, 2004 ... The complaint alleged that Marietta College (College) excluded a former student (Student), from participation in its academic program on the basis of disability. Specifically, the complaint alleged that, after a psychologist on staff at the College shared information about the Student's disability (depression) and history of suicide attempts with a College Dean, the College determined that the Student was a threat to himself and dismissed him on September 19, 2004.

OCR is responsible for enforcing Section 504 of the Rehabilitation Act of 1973 ... The College is a recipient of Federal financial assistance from the Department. OCR, therefore, has jurisdiction over this complaint ...

Based on a careful analysis ... OCR determined that the College's actions in this situation did not comply with the requirements of the Section 504 regulation. However, the College has agreed to take action to resolve the compliance issues raised during this investigation. The basis for OCR's determination is discussed below.

The Student was admitted to the College as a freshman for its fall 2004 term. Before the College's academic year began in August 2004, the Student and his parents attended the College's Summer Schedule Days, which is an annual College activity held for students to schedule classes and to orient students and parents to the College. During this time, the Dean of Student Life (Dean) conducted a session for parents on College resources. The Dean indicated that, after this session, the Student's parents spoke to him about the type of counseling services the College offered, indicating that the Student would need counseling once he began attending the College. The Dean advised them to contact the College's psychologist.

The Student's mother then called the psychologist in mid-August to request counseling services for the Student. During that conversation, she told the psychologist that the Student had attempted suicide in spring 2003 and gave the psychologist consent to speak to the Student's psychiatrist in New York. The psychologist later contacted the Student's parents and asked to meet with them without the Student during their planned visit to the College for a parents' weekend so that he could better understand the Student's needs. The Student's father indicated that when they met with the psychologist on September 18, however, they realized that the psychologist had shared with the College administration information about the Student's depression and past suicide attempts. According to the Student's parents, the College then used that information to involuntarily dismiss the Student from the College, after he had only been a student there for approximately one month, based on the Student's depression and history of suicide attempts.

Pursuant to the Section 504 implementing regulation, at 34 C.F.R. §104.3(j)(l), an individual with a disability is any person who has a physical or mental impairment which substantially limits one or more major life activities, has a record of such an impairment, or is regarded as having such an impairment ... Pursuant to 34 C.F.R. §104.43, no qualified student with a disability shall, on the basis of disability, be excluded from participation in, be denied the benefits of, or otherwise be subjected to discrimination under any postsecondary education program ...

The Student met the academic standards required for admission to the College. The College also acknowledged that it was aware of the Student's depression and past suicide attempts. The College does not dispute that, pursuant to its Emergency Withdrawal Policy, it involuntarily dismissed the Student from its program on September 19, 2004. The College contends, however, that its dismissal of the Student was legitimate and not discriminatory because information that the College had gathered about the Student through its psychologist supported that the Student posed a direct threat to himself.

Although Section 504 does not prohibit a postsecondary education institution from taking action to address an imminent risk of danger posed by an individual with a disability who represents a direct threat to the health and safety of himself/herself or others, such action must be grounded in sound evidence and cannot be based on unfounded fears, prejudice, or stereotypes regarding individuals with psychiatric disabilities to ensure that such individuals are not discriminated against because of their disability. *To rise to the level of a direct threat, there must be a high probability of substantial harm and not just a slightly increased, speculative, or remote risk.*

In a direct threat situation, a postsecondary education institution needs to make an individualized and objective assessment of the student's ability to safely participate in the institution's program based on a reasonable medical judgment relying on the most current medical knowledge or the best available objective evidence. The assessment must determine the nature, duration, and severity of the risk; the probability that the potentially threatening injury will actually occur; and whether reasonable modifications of policies, practices, or procedures will sufficiently mitigate the risk. Due process requires a postsecondary institution to adhere to procedures that ensure that students with disabilities are not subject to adverse action on the basis of unfounded fear, prejudice, or stereotypes. A nondiscriminatory belief must be based on observation of a student's conduct, actions, and statements, not merely knowledge or beliefs that a student is an individual with a disability.

In exceptional circumstances, such as situations where safety is of immediate concern, a college may take interim steps pending a final decision regarding an adverse action against a student as long as minimal due process, such as notice and an opportunity to address the evidence, is provided in the interim and full due process, including a hearing and the right to appeal, is offered later.

Because the College asserted a direct threat defense in support of its dismissal of the Student, OCR gathered evidence from the College regarding its decision to dismiss the Student and analyzed it applying the direct threat principles stated above. The College indicated that it based its decision on information provided by its psychologist. The psychologist first expressed concerns to the Dean about the Student on September 14. At that time, the psychologist indicated that his concerns were that the Student seemed evasive and uncooperative during his first counseling session with him on August 26 and was not interested in having counseling sessions more than once or twice a month. This concerned the psychologist because, according to him, the Student's New York psychiatrist stressed to him during a telephone conversation that the Student needed weekly counseling and cautioned that the Student does not give any warning before his suicide attempts.

In addition, the psychologist had reviewed records obtained from the psychiatrist that described the Student's depression and suicidal tendencies. The psychologist also indicated that the Student's Resident Dorm Director contacted him in early September to advise that the Student's roommate had reported that the Student was acting strangely and frequently talked about death ...

On the same day that the psychologist spoke to the Dean, the psychologist told OCR that he saw the Student on campus and approached him to ask why the Student had not contacted him since their first session. He stated that the Student responded by saying that he was fine and that he felt that meeting more than once a month was unnecessary; however, the Student agreed to meet with the psychologist a second time on September 16. The psychologist stated that he called the New York psychiatrist to advise her that the Student was avoiding therapy, and she again stressed that the Student needed weekly counseling and that, if he did not want to meet with the psychologist, to try and get him off-campus counseling. The psychologist indicated he reported this conversation to the Dean and made unsuccessful attempts to identify an off-campus psychiatrist for the Student.

Finally, the psychologist stated that during his second session with the Student on September 16, the Student boasted that if he was going to commit suicide again no one would ever know and advised the psychologist of a third suicide attempt that the Student claimed no one knew about. After this second session, the psychologist went to the Dean and expressed his concern that the Student's statements during that session constituted a veiled threat to kill himself. Based on this information, the College decided to suggest in the meeting with the parents two days later that the Student voluntarily withdraw based on medical need and that, if the Student did not agree to withdraw voluntarily, the College would exercise its emergency involuntary withdrawal policy, which provides that Students who threaten or attempt suicide may be involuntarily withdrawn from the College.

The College indicated that the parents rejected the College's offer to voluntarily withdraw the Student for medical need at their meeting on September 18 so that when they met with the Student and his parents the next day, the College advised them that they were involuntarily withdrawing the Student from the College. The parents objected but were told by the College that the action might only be temporary if they, as a condition of the Student's return, provided documentation that the Student was seeing a qualified mental health professional and that he was mentally stable. In addition, the Student would have to agree to a behavior contract upon his return. The parents indicated that they would not agree to these conditions because they did not believe the College should be dismissing the Student and that the Student would not return. As a result, the College refunded the Student's tuition and room and board . . .

During its investigation, OCR determined that the decision to involuntarily withdraw the Student from the College was based on a discussion between the Dean, the College President, and the College's legal counsel, based on the information provided by the College's psychologist . . .

Although the psychologist's interactions with the Student may have given the College some grounds for concern about how the Student was adapting to College life, OCR finds that the information was not sufficient to demonstrate the existence of the type of high probability of substantial harm to the Student, as opposed to a slightly increased or speculative risk, necessary to support a direct threat defense. In total, the psychologist met with the Student for two one-hour sessions. The College never conducted an individualized and objective assessment of the Student's ability to safely participate in the College's program, based on a reasonable medical judgment, and did not consider whether the perceived risk of injury to the Student could have been mitigated by reasonable modifications of College policies, practices, or procedures.

Also, although the College offered the parents the opportunity to provide information regarding the Student's proposed treatment plan and mental stability as conditions for a possible return to the College, *the parents were never explicitly advised of their right to appeal and challenge the dismissal decision itself. Furthermore, OCR's investigation revealed that the College does not have a grievance procedure for disability discrimination complaints* or a Section 504 coordinator as required by the Section 504 regulation at 34 C.F.R. 104.37.

On March 18, 2005, the College voluntarily agreed to implement [an] agreement to resolve the compliance issues identified during the complaint investigation. Pursuant to the agreement, the College will designate a responsible employee to serve as its Section 504 coordinator and publish the name or title and contact information for that employee on a continuing basis in its recruitment materials and general publications, including its Student Handbook; send an offer of readmission to the Student for the 2005-2006 school year; *amend its Emergency Withdrawal Policy to include language that makes clear that a decision to subject a student with a disability to an emergency withdrawal will be made in consultation with persons knowledgeable about the College's obligations under Federal disability civil rights laws and direct threat standards, including the College's Section 504 Coordinator, and with appropriate medical or other professionals; amend its Emergency Withdrawal Policy to ensure that it contains language that complies with current law on when the College can involuntarily withdraw a student with a disability; amend its Emergency Withdrawal Policy to include conditions for a student's re-*

turn to the College after an emergency withdrawal, consistent with Federal disability laws and with consideration of the individual circumstances of each student; develop and notify students and staff of grievance procedures that provide for prompt and equitable complaint resolution for disability discrimination complaints; and provide training to its Section 504 coordinator about the College's obligations to students with disabilities under Section 504, including proper implementation and administration of its Emergency Withdrawal Policy and procedures. OCR will monitor the implementation of the agreement. If the College fails to fully implement the agreement, OCR will reopen the complaint.

Based on the above, we are closing this complaint effective the date of this letter. OCR appreciates the courtesy and cooperation shown by your staff and legal counsel during the investigation and resolution of this complaint. We look forward to receiving your first monitoring report, which is due on September 22, 2005 . . .

Appendix C

Two Competing Views on the Duty of Care

JAIN V. STATE OF IOWA

No "Special Relationship" in Student Suicide Cases

Jain v. State of Iowa 617 N.W.2d 293 (Iowa 2000). Excerpts in "question and answer" format:

What are the facts of the case?

Sanjay Jain had just celebrated his eighteenth birthday when he enrolled as a freshman at the University of Iowa and moved into an off-campus university dormitory, the Mayflower. Sanjay came to Iowa from Addison, Illinois, the second of three children born to Uttam and Anita Jain. By all accounts they were a close-knit family.

Sanjay had enjoyed a successful academic career in high school and planned to major in biomedical engineering at the university. That course of study proved difficult. By the middle of the first semester his personal life as well as academic performance were showing the strain. He became moody and skipped many classes. He experimented with drugs and alcohol. In early November he was involved in an egg-throwing incident at the dormitory. He was penalized with three hours of compulsory community service. Soon after he was placed on one-year disciplinary probation for smoking marijuana in his room.

Beth Merritt, the hall coordinator for the Mayflower dorm, imposed this discipline and ordered him to attend a series of alcohol and drug education classes. Sanjay's parents and family were unaware of these difficulties. University policy calls for privacy with respect to the university's relationships with its adult students.

Although Sanjay confided to his mother that he wished to switch his major from engineering to computer science, he told his father and brother that he liked biomedical engineering and his classes were going well. His frequent phone conversations with his parents were reportedly upbeat. Sanjay, in his father's words, described everything about college as "awesome."

In the early morning hours of November 20, 1994, resident assistants on duty at the Mayflower were called to a "domestic" dispute outside Sanjay's apartment. When they arrived they observed Sanjay and his girlfriend, Roopa, fighting over a set of keys to Sanjay's moped. Sanjay had moved the motorized cycle into his room. Roopa asserted that Sanjay was preparing to commit suicide by inhaling exhaust fumes and she was merely trying to stop him. Sanjay was interviewed independently. He, too, reported that he was trying to commit suicide. The RAs concluded from their conversation that Sanjay "had a lot of frustrations about family life and academics." After discussing the situation for about an hour, the group disbanded. Sanjay assured the RAs that he would seek counseling after getting a good night's rest.

Beth Merritt met with Sanjay the next day. He was reportedly evasive and refused to admit or deny that he had tried to commit suicide. She encouraged him to seek help at the university counseling service. She also demanded that he remove the moped from his room because storing it there violated university policy. He agreed to do so. Merritt also gave Sanjay her home phone number, urging him to call her "if he thought he was going to hurt himself." Sanjay assured her he would do so. He reportedly claimed that he just really needed to talk to his family and looked forward to doing so during the Thanksgiving break that would start the next day.

In keeping with university protocol, Merritt discussed the Sanjay incident with her supervisor, David Coleman, the assistant director for residence life. She expressed concern that the RA's incident report stated "Sanjay was trying to commit suicide by inhaling fumes of his scooter in an unventilated room" while Sanjay insisted the report "wasn't exactly the truth." She told Coleman that her personal conversation with Sanjay revealed more tiredness on his part than hopelessness or despair. She also advised Coleman that she requested permission to contact Sanjay's parents about the incident, but he refused to consent. Coleman concurred in Merritt's decision to encourage Sanjay to seek counseling. He took no further action on the matter.

Evidently Sanjay's visit with his family at Thanksgiving did not include discussion of the turmoil in his life. His parents and siblings perceived nothing amiss in his attitude or behavior. Sanjay returned to the university when classes resumed on November 28. Merritt encountered him briefly and inquired about how things were going. Sanjay responded "good." Unbeknownst to Merritt, however, the moped was back in Sanjay's room. In a statement given after Sanjay's death, his roommate, Scott, reported that the vehicle had been stored in

Sanjay's room for roughly three weeks. Sanjay reportedly told Scott that "he would kill himself by running the cycle in the room . . . when Scott was not there."

This threat, apparently taken in jest by Scott, played out on December 4. Scott planned to spend the weekend in Cedar Rapids. Sanjay called his brother to make arrangements for a ride home over the upcoming winter break, then joined friends for a night of drinking downtown. They stayed until the bars closed at 2 a.m. Sanjay was described as "visibly intoxicated but coherent . . ."

At approximately 10:30 a.m., one of Sanjay's suite-mates awoke to the smell of something "unusual." He ignored it but, thirty minutes later, he felt dizzy when he tried to get up. He suspected the pilot light might have gone out on the apartment's stove. When he opened the door to the kitchen a cloud of exhaust smoke appeared there and in the bathroom. Fearing another suicide attempt by Sanjay, he knocked on his door but received no answer. All he heard was loud music coming from the room. He contacted the RA on duty, who unlocked the door and found Sanjay unconscious, the moped still running. Emergency medical personnel were summoned and the dormitory was evacuated. Sanjay was pronounced dead of self-inflicted carbon monoxide poisoning.

Was there a university policy regarding notice to parents?

The record reveals that an unwritten university policy dealing with self-destructive behavior dictates that, with evidence of a suicide attempt, university officials will contact a student's parents. The decision to do so rests solely with Phillip Jones, the dean of students. The dean bases his decision on information gathered from a variety of sources. In this case, no information concerning Sanjay Jain was transmitted to the dean's office until after his death.

What is the plaintiff's legal claim?

At the outset plaintiff concedes that the law generally imposes no duty upon an individual to protect another person from self-inflicted harm in the absence of a "special relationship," usually custodial in nature. Restatement (Second) of Torts §314, at 116 (1965); see *Cutler v. Klass, Whicher & Mishne*, 473 N.W.2d 178, 182 (Iowa 1991) (noting narrow exception to traditional rule in the case of jails or hospitals); *Nally v. Grace Community Church of the Valley*, 763 P.2d 948, 956 (Cal. 1988) (same); *McLaughlin v. Sullivan*, 461 A.2d 123, 125 (N.H. 1983) (same). Plaintiff claims no reliance on the "custody or control" exception here, conceding the university's relationship with its students is not custodial in nature. What plaintiff does claim is that the university's knowledge of Sanjay's "mental condition or emotional state requiring medical care" created a special relationship giving rise to an affirmative duty of care toward him.

Plaintiff's focus is on the Restatement (Second) of Torts section 323. It states:

> One who undertakes, gratuitously or for consideration, to render services to another which he should recognize as necessary for the protection of the other's person or things, is subject to liability to the other for physical harm resulting from his failure to exercise reasonable care to perform his undertaking, if
>
> (a) his failure to exercise such care increases the risk of such harm, or
>
> (b) the harm is suffered because of the other's reliance upon the undertaking.

[The plaintiff] posits two possible circumstances that could establish the university's special duty to Sanjay under this record: (1) its adherence to an exception in federal legislation known as the "Buckley Amendment" that otherwise protects the confidentiality of student records, or (2) the university's adoption of a policy to notify parents of a student's self-destructive behavior ...

Does the Buckley Amendment create a duty to warn parents?

Congress enacted the Family Educational Rights and Privacy Act (FERPA) to ensure access to educational records for students and parents while protecting the privacy of such records from the public ... At issue here is an exception that permits institutions to disclose otherwise confidential information to "appropriate parties" when an "emergency" makes it necessary "to protect the health or safety of the student or other persons ..." A companion regulation directs that the exception be "strictly construed ..."

Jain contends an emergency existed with respect to his son, Sanjay, and it was vitally important for Sanjay's parents to have information concerning the situation so they could intervene on his behalf. He then seems to argue that because the exception to the Buckley Amendment would have authorized revelation of the pertinent facts, the university was duty bound to reveal them ...

We entertain serious doubts about the merits of plaintiff's argument. His claim rests, after all, not on a violation of the Act but on an alleged failure to take advantage of a discretionary exception to its requirements. We need not resolve the question, however, because plaintiff has not preserved the issue for our review. His claim that the university wrongfully withheld information "under the guise of the Buckley Amendment" was neither raised before the [lower] court nor ruled upon in its decision. As a result we give the contention no further consideration ...

Did the university assume a duty to notify parents?

[T]he crux of the Plaintiff's claim [is] that the university has voluntarily adopted a policy (consistent with the Buckley Amendment) of notifying parents when a student engages in self-destructive behavior but it negligently failed to act on that policy in the case of Sanjay Jain. By not following its own policy, plaintiff argues, the "university deprived Sanjay of the medical intervention he so desperately needed."

The argument implicates section 323 of the *Restatement (Second) of Torts*. Although this court has applied section 323 in a variety of settings, we have not before had occasion to consider the rule's application in the context of an allegedly preventable death by suicide . . .

Cases interpreting section 323(a) have made it clear that the increase in the risk of harm required is not simply that which occurs when a person fails to do something that he or she reasonably should have. Obviously, the risk of harm to the beneficiary of a service is always greater when the service is performed without due care. Rather, as the court stated in *Turbe v.Government of Virgin Islands, Virgin Island Water & Power Auth.*, 939 F.2d 427, 432 (3d Cir. 1991):

> [Section] 323(a) applies only when the defendant's actions increased the risk of harm to plaintiff relative to the risk that would have existed had the defendant never provided the services initially. Put another way, the defendant's negligent performance must somehow put the plaintiff in a worse situation than if the defendant had never begun performance . . . [T]o prevail under a theory of increased harm a plaintiff must "identify the sins of commission rather than sins of omission."

Likewise with respect to the "reliance" prong of section 323(b), the *Power* court noted the general requirement that the plaintiff show "actual or affirmative reliance, i.e., reliance 'based on specific actions or representations which cause a person to forego other alternatives of protecting themselves . . .'"

Plaintiff argues, in essence, that once university employees discovered Sanjay and Roopa fighting over the moped keys, elicited comments suggestive of a suicide threat and referred Sanjay to counseling, they were bound under section 323 to follow through with their undertaking. In this case, plaintiff argues, that meant bringing the matter to the attention of the dean of students for the purpose of notifying Sanjay's parents.

Although, in hindsight, plaintiff's contention carries considerable appeal, the duty he seeks to impose upon the university cannot be squared with section 323(a) or (b). The record, read in the light most favorable to the plaintiff, reveals that Sanjay may have been at risk of harming himself. No affirmative action by the defendant's employees, however, increased that risk of self-harm. To the contrary, it is undisputed that the RAs appropriately intervened in an emotionally-charged situation, offered Sanjay support and encouragement, and referred him to counseling. Beth Merritt likewise counseled Sanjay to talk things over with his parents, seek professional help, and call her at any time . . . She sought Sanjay's permission to contact his parents but he refused. In short, no action by university personnel prevented Sanjay from taking advantage of the help and encouragement being offered, nor did they do anything to prevent him from seeking help on his own accord.

The record is similarly devoid of any proof that Sanjay relied, to his detriment, on the services gratuitously offered by these same personnel. To the contrary, it appears by all accounts that he failed to follow up on recommended counseling or seek the guidance of his parents, as he assured the staff he would do . . .

This case is distinctly different from the only case relied upon by plaintiff in support of his section 323 argument, *United States v. Gavagan*, 280 F.2d 319 (5th Cir. 1960). *Gavagan* involved the question of governmental liability for the unsuccessful rescue of a ship in distress at sea . . . Although plaintiff understandably looks to the case as a metaphor for the failed rescue perceived in the case before us, the court's affirmance of a verdict for the estates of the deceased crew members in *Gavagan* turned on proof of the essential elements of Restatement section 323. The case reveals that but for negligent mistakes in the conveyance of vital information concerning the vessel's location, lives lost would have been saved . . . Crucial to the court's decision was proof that the mistakes greatly increased the likelihood that the ship would not be found before dark, and reliance on the misleading information led others to abandon their search.

By contrast to *Gavagan*, the record before us reveals that the university's limited intervention in this case neither increased the risk that Sanjay would commit suicide nor led him to abandon other avenues of relief from his distress. Thus no legal duty on the part of the university arose under Restatement section 323 as a matter of law.

What is the general rule concerning liability for suicide?

In Iowa and elsewhere, it is the general rule that unless the possibility of accident or innocence can be reasonably determined, the act of suicide is considered a deliberate, intentional and intervening act that precludes another's responsibility for the harm. *Cutler*, 473 N.W.2d at 182; *McLaughlin*, 461 A.2d at 124; *Falkenstein v. City of Bismarck*, 268 N.W.2d 787, 790 (N.D. 1978); *W. Page Keeton, Prosser and Keeton on the Law of Torts* §44, at 311 (5th ed. 1984). As already noted earlier in this opinion, an exception to this general rule arises from the existence of a special relationship that imposes upon the defen-

dant the duty to prevent foreseeable harm to the plaintiff. *Cutler*, 473
N.W.2d at 182. In such a case, the doctrine of intervening-superseding
act will not relieve a defendant of liability. *Stevens by Stevens v. Des
Moines Indep. Community Sch. Dist.*, 528 N.W.2d 117, 119 (Iowa 1995).
That is because the intervening act (in this case, suicide) is the very
risk the special duty is meant to prevent . . .

Here, the district court logically concluded that because no legally-
recognized special relationship existed between the university and Sanjay, plaintiff could not rely on the exception to the intervening-
superseding cause doctrine to counter the university's affirmative defense. We agree. Accordingly we affirm the district court's summary
judgment for the State of Iowa.

LAVERNE F. SCHIESZLER V. FERRUM COLLEGE

Duty of care to prevent suicide

Laverne F. Schieszler v. Ferrum College 236 F. Supp. 2d 602 (W.D.
Va. 2002). Excerpts in question and answer format:

What are the facts of the case?

This wrongful death suit arises out of the suicide of Michael Frentzel. At the time of his death, Frentzel was a freshman at Ferrum College. His first semester at college was apparently not an entirely happy
experience. As a result of some undisclosed "disciplinary issues," Ferrum required Frentzel to comply with certain conditions before permitting him to continue his enrollment. Among these was the
requirement that Frentzel enroll in anger management counseling before
returning for the spring semester.

Frentzel apparently complied with these conditions and returned
to Ferrum for a second semester. On February 20, 2000, Frentzel had
an argument with his girlfriend, Crystal. The campus police and the
resident assistant at Frentzel's on-campus dormitory, Odessa Holley,
responded and intervened. At around the same time, Frentzel sent
a note to Crystal in which he indicated that he intended to hang himself with his belt. Holley and the campus police were shown the note.
When they responded, they found Frentzel locked in his room. When
they managed to get into his room, the found Frentzel with bruises
on his head. He told them the bruises were self-inflicted. The campus
police informed Ferrum's dean of student affairs, David Newcombe,
about the incident. Newcombe responded by requiring Frentzel to sign
a statement that he would not hurt himself. Newcombe then left Frentzel alone to go speak with Crystal.

Within the next few days, Frentzel wrote another note to a friend
stating "tell Crystal I will always love her." The friend told Crystal
who told the defendants. They refused to allow her to return to Frent-

zel's dormitory room. The defendants took no other action. Soon thereafter, Frentzel wrote yet another note stating "only God can help me now," which Crystal pressed upon the defendants. When the defendants visited Frentzel's room on February 23, 2002, they found that he had hung himself with his belt.

What is the legal issue?

Frentzel's aunt and guardian, LaVerne Schieszler, was named the personal representative of his estate in Illinois. She filed a wrongful death suit against Ferrum College, Newcombe, and Holley. The complaint alleges a single count of wrongful death ... It avers that the defendants "knew or personally should have known that Frentzel was likely to attempt to hurt himself if not properly supervised," that they were "negligent by failing to take adequate precautions to insure that Frentzel did not hurt himself," and that Frentzel died as a result.

The defendants have jointly moved to dismiss this complaint, arguing that ... a claim for wrongful death will not lie because Frentzel's suicide was an unlawful act; [that] the defendants had no legal duty to take steps to prevent Frentzel from killing himself; and ... the defendants' actions were not the cause of Frentzel's death ...

How is duty defined?

In her claim for wrongful death, the plaintiff alleges that the defendants were negligent in failing to take adequate steps to prevent Frentzel from committing suicide ... Ordinarily, there is no affirmative duty to act to assist or protect another absent unusual circumstances, which justify imposing such an affirmative responsibility. Under Section 314A of the *Restatement (Second) of Torts* (1965), an affirmative duty to aid or protect will arise when a special relationship exists between the parties. Section 314A identifies a number of special relationships, including the relationship between a common carrier and its passengers, an innkeeper and his guests, a possessor of land and his invitees, and one who takes custody of another thereby depriving him of other assistance. The special relationships listed in the Restatement are not considered exclusive. *Restatement (Second) of Torts* 314A cmt. b (1965) ("The relations listed are not intended to be exclusive.")

Virginia law similarly recognizes that a special relationship can give rise to a duty to take affirmative action to assist or protect another ... The Virginia Supreme Court has held that a special relationship exists as a matter of law between a common carrier and its passengers, an employer and his employees, an innkeeper an his guests and a business owner and his invitees ... These are not the only relationships that will give rise to an affirmative duty to assist or protect. The Court also has recognized that a special relationship may exist between particular plaintiffs and defendants because of the par-

82   *Questions and Answers on College Student Suicide ...*

ticular factual circumstances in a given case, See *Thompson* [*v.Skate America*] 540 S.E.2d [123] at 127 ("[S]pecial relationships may exist between particular plaintiffs and defendants, either as a matter of law or because of the particular factual circumstances in a given case."); *Delk v. Columbia/HCA Healthcare Corp.*, 523 S.E.2d 826, 830-31 (2000) (medical facility created de facto special relationship with its patient when it determined she was in need of constant supervision and surveillance); *Burdette v. Marks*, 421 S.E.2d 419, 420-21 (1992)(special relationship existed between deputy and passerby which imposed legal duty upon deputy to render assistance to passerby and protect him from attack).

In *Burdette v. Marks*, 421 S.E.2d 419, (1992), for example, the Court considered whether a special relationship existed between a police officer and a passerby such that the officer had a duty to protect the passerby from an attack. In determining whether such a special relationship existed, the Court "consider[ed] whether [the officer] could reasonably have foreseen that he would be expected to take affirmative action to protect [the passerby] from harm . . ." The Court noted that the officer was present when the passerby was attacked; the officer was on duty at the time, from which it could be inferred that he was armed and able to intervene without exposing himself to undue danger; the officer knew the passerby was in great danger; and the passerby asked for help . . . The Court concluded that a special relationship existed "based upon the particular facts alleged . . ."

In the case most similar to this one, *Commercial Distributors v. Blakenship*, 397 S.E.2d 840, 846 (1990), the Virginia Supreme Court concluded that a residential facility had a duty to protect its mentally disabled residents while they were on the premises. In doing so, the Court did not expressly conclude that a special relationship existed between a facility and its residents. The Court also found that the facility's duty was not as extensive as that of a hospital, nursing home or other custodial institution . . . Nonetheless, the Court indicated that, had the plaintiff's decedent, a resident who committed suicide, been on the premises at the time of his death, and had his suicide been foreseeable, the facility would have had a duty to take steps to assist him.

Is there a special relationship between a university and a student?

The Virginia Supreme Court has not yet addressed the issue of whether a special relationship may arise between a University and a student. In a case arising under Virginia law, the Fourth Circuit has concluded that "[a school's] acceptance of a student with special problems created a corresponding duty to take reasonable steps to cope with the problems." *Seidman v. Fishburne-Hudgins Ed. Found.*, 724 F.2d 413, 418 (1984). *Seidman* involved a private boarding school, which, upon dismissing a troubled student, returned his personal items, including a firearm. The student shot himself immediately thereafter.

Thus, the Fourth Circuit found a duty to protect under facts very similar to the facts in this case. Beyond its conclusion that the school had a duty to protect the student, however, the court did not discuss whether a special relationship existed between the school and the student or whether the duty arose from such a relationship. Moreover, this case can be distinguished because *Seidman* involved a minor. Because the student in *Seidman* was a minor, the Fourth Circuit may simply have presumed that the school stood *in loco parentis* to the student, and that a special relationship therefore existed. The instant case does not involve a minor, and therefore, strictly speaking, no duty arises from an *in loco parentis* relationship between Ferrum and Frentzel.

I can find no cases in other jurisdictions, and the parties have proffered none, that address whether a special relationship exists under the facts presented in this case. The defendants point to two cases, *Jain v. Iowa*, 617 N.W.2d 293 (2000), and *Bogust v. Iverson*, 10 Wis.2d 129, 102 N.W.2d 228 (1960). Neither of these cases are helpful because they do not address whether a special relationship exists between school an student. Rather, both cases consider liability under *Restatement (Second) of Torts* 323 (1965), a theory the plaintiff in this case abandoned at oral argument.

A number of cases in recent years have considered whether colleges and universities have a duty to take steps to protect students who voluntarily become intoxicated. See *Bradshaw v. Rawlings,* 612 F.2d 135 (3d Cir. 1979) (finding no special relationship); *Coghlan v. Beta Theta Pi Fraternity,* 987, P.2d 300 (1999) (same); *Univ. of Denver v. Whitlock,* 744 P.2d 54 (Colo. 1987)(same); *Beach v. University of Utah,* 726 P.2d 413, 416 (Utah 1986) (same); see also *Furek v. University of Delaware,* 594 A.2d 506, 522 (Del.1991) (finding no special relationship giving rise to duty to protect student from hazing injuries).

In the vast bulk of these cases, courts have concluded that no special relationship existed. Underlying the analysis in these cases is the conclusion that the school could not have foreseen that the student was in danger. In *Beach v. University of Utah,* for example, the Utah Supreme Court concluded that no special relationship existed because nothing University personnel knew would have led them to conclude that the plaintiff might be injured. 726 P.2d 413, 416 (1986). In *Furek v. University of Delaware,* the court acknowledged that no duty arose merely from the school-student relationship, but concluded that when a college or university knows of danger to its students, it has a duty to aid or protect them. 594 A2d 506, 519-520 (Del.1991).

Is there another basis to find a legal duty?

The conclusion that the relationship between a college or university and its students can give rise to a duty to protect students from harms of which the school has knowledge is consistent with the Virginia Supreme Court's analysis in other contexts. In the recently decided *Thompson v. Skate America, Inc.* 540 S.E.2d 123, 127 (2001), a case involving the duty of [a] landowner to protect his invitees, the Court concluded that special relationships may exist between particular plaintiffs and defendants because of the factual circumstances of a case. In addition, the Court's analysis has placed particular emphasis on the forseeability of the harm. Under the Court's precedents, the existence of a special relationship will not, standing alone, give rise to a duty; the harm must be foreseeable ...

In *Wright v. Webb*, [362 S.E. 2d 919, 921 (1987)] the Court held that an affirmative duty to assist or protect will not arise unless the defendant knew there was "an imminent probability of harm ..." Wright involved a suit against motel owners for injuries sustained by an invitee as a result of being assaulted in the motel's parking lot ... "In determining whether a duty exists," the Court stated, "the likelihood of injury, the magnitude of the burden of guarding against it, and the consequences of placing that burden on the defendant must be taken into account ..." The court concluded that prior crimes committed on the premises of the motel did not give the defendant notice of a "specific" or "imminent" danger. *Id.* at 533. Accordingly, the Court held that the motel owners had no duty to assist or protect their invitee ...

Did the college have a duty in this case?

While it is unlikely that Virginia would conclude that a special relationship exists as a matter of law between colleges and universities and their students, it might find that a special relationship exists on the particular facts alleged in this case. Frentzel was a full-time student at Ferrum College. He lived in an on-campus dormitory. The defendants were aware that Frentzel had emotional problems; they had required him to seek anger management counseling before permitting him to return to school for a second semester. The defendants knew that, within days of his death, Frentzel was found by campus police alone in his room with bruises on his head and that he claimed these bruises were self-inflicted. The defendants knew that, at around the same time, Frentzel had sent a message to his girlfriend, in which he stated that he intended to kill himself. The defendants knew that Frentzel had sent other communications, to his girlfriend and to another friend, suggesting that he intended to kill himself.

After Frentzel was found alone in his room with bruises on his head, the defendants required Frentzel to sign a statement that he would not hurt himself. This last fact, more than any other, indicates that the defendants believed Frentzel was likely to harm himself. Based on these alleged facts, a trier of fact could conclude that there was "an imminent probability" that Frentzel would try to hurt himself, and that the defendants had notice of this specific harm. Thus, I find that the plaintiff has alleged sufficient facts to support her claim that a special relationship existed between Frentzel and defendants giving rise to a duty to protect Frentzel from the foreseeable danger that he would hurt himself.

In reaching this conclusion, I have also considered whether defendants could reasonably have foreseen that they would be expected to take affirmative action to assist Frentzel. See *Burdette v. Marks*, 421 S.E.2d 419 (1992)("In determining whether such a special relationship existed, it is important to consider whether [the defendant] reasonably could have foreseen that he would be expected to take affirmative action to protect [the plaintiff]."). It is true that colleges are not insurers of the safety of their students. See *Coghlan v. Beta Theta Pi Fraternity*, 987 P2d 300, 312 (1999). It is also true that Ferrum did not technically stand *in loco parentis* vis-a-vis Frentzel and his fellow students. Nonetheless, "[p]arents, students, and the general community still have a reasonable expectation, fostered in part by colleges themselves, that reasonable care will be exercised to protect resident students from foreseeable harm." *Mullins v. Pine Manor College*, 449 N.E.2d 331 (1983).

The plaintiff also has alleged sufficient facts to support her allegation that defendants Ferrum and Newcombe breached a duty to assist Frentzel. According to the facts alleged in the complaint, after finding Frentzel alone in his room with bruises on his head, Frentzel was left alone. After Frentzel sent the message to his girlfriend suggesting that he might hurt himself, the defendants responded by refusing to permit her to return to his room. According to the complaint, they took no steps to ensure that Frentzel was supervised or to contact his guardian. They failed to obtain counseling for him even though they had previously required him to undergo counseling. They took no other steps. That said, the facts alleged do not indicate that defendant Holley, the resident assistant at Frentzel's dormitory, could have taken any additional steps to aid or protect Frentzel absent some direction from Ferrum or Newcombe. Thus, I find, that under the facts alleged, only Ferrum and Newcombe could have breached their duty tor render assistance to Frentzel. The claim against defendant Holley is therefore dismissed.

The defendants contend this case is different from the cases cited above because Frentzel committed suicide. Admittedly, most of the cases in which the Virginia Supreme Court has discussed an affirmative duty to protect or assist have involved harm caused by a third party, not harm caused by one's self ... [But] [t]he Court in no way indicated that it intended to limit the circumstances under which a duty would arise to protect or assist a person who is suicidal.

Were the college's acts or omissions the cause of the suicide?

Next, the defendants contend that the complaint fails to allege facts from which a trier of fact could find that their acts or omissions proximately caused Frentzel's suicide. Negligent breach of a duty is actionable only when it constitutes a proximate cause of the injury ... Ordinarily, however, questions of proximate cause are not decided on a notion to dismiss. ... They only become a question of law if the facts alleged are susceptible of only one inference ...

In Virginia, an injury is proximately caused by a defendant's negligence if the injury is the natural and probable consequence of the negligence ... The natural and probable consequences are those which human foresight can foresee ...

Keeping in mind that proximate cause is a question of fact unless the facts alleged are susceptible of only one inference ... I cannot find at this early stage of the proceedings that the defendants' alleged failure to take steps to aid Frentzel was not a proximate cause of his death. The plaintiff has alleged that the defendants had been told that Frentzel had more than once threatened to kill himself and that he had already injured himself once. Thus, the facts alleged in the complaint indicate that the risk that Frentzel would in fact take his own life was foreseeable. Although the defendants had at their disposal campus police, the College's counseling services and the resident assistant in Frentzel's dormitory, the plaintiff alleges that they took no steps to ensure that Frentzel was supervised.

In addition, according to the plaintiff's amended complaint, the defendants did not contact Frentzel's guardian and refused to permit Frentzel's girlfriend to return to his room after he threatened to injure himself. Instead, the defendants left Frentzel alone. While alone, in his room, Frentzel hung himself. According to the complaint, all of these events occurred within a three day period. In view of these alleged facts, I cannot say as a matter of law that Frentzel's suicide was not a foreseeable result of the defendants failure to ensure that Frentzel was supervised.

Can plaintiff recover for the illegal act of suicide?

Lastly, the defendants contend that the plaintiff is barred from recovering for wrongful death because Frentzel's death was caused by suicide, an illegal act. In general, a plaintiff may not recover for an injury received as the result of another's negligence if the plaintiff voluntarily was involved in an illegal act at the time the injury occurred ... However, the Virginia Supreme Court has held that if the illegal act in question is the victim's suicide, and the suicide was the result of the victim being of unsound mind at the time of his death, the defense of illegality will not bar recovery for wrongful death. See *Molchon v. Tyler*, 262 Va. 175, 181 (2001); ... In *Molchon*, a personal representative sued his decedent's psychiatrist who had released the decedent from hospital care after diagnosing him with acute depression and suicidal tendencies; the decedent thereafter committed suicide ...

The Virginia Supreme Court concluded that the personal representative could bring a wrongful death action against the psychiatrist. *Id.* In her Amended complaint, Schieszler alleges that Frentzel "was not of sound mind at the time he took his own life." In support of this legal conclusion, she alleges that Ferrum required Michael to enter counseling as a condition of his continued enrollment and that he had threatened suicide and physically injured himself in the days before his death. I find that the plaintiff has sufficiently alleged that Frentzel was of unsound mind at the time of his death. Thus, the fact that Frentzel's death was caused by suicide will not bar recovery for wrongful death at this stage of the proceedings.

Appendix D

Student Suicide Law & Policy Perspectives:
Advice to residence life staff members.

By Gary Pavela

[1] Is the student suicide rate increasing?

No. Public attention to a crisis sometimes intensifies after the crisis has peaked. In the case of completed suicides among teenagers and young adults, national data show a decline in suicide rates beginning in the early 1990s. The current downward trend, however, comes after a tripling of the youth suicide rate between 1950 and 1994. Youth suicide constitutes what the Centers for Disease Control and Prevention (CDC) calls "a major public health problem" in the United States— and remains the third leading cause of death in the 15-24 age group, after unintentional injuries and homicide.

News accounts of individual incidents sometimes create the impression that college students are more likely to commit suicide than their non-college attending peers. Researchers agree, however, that college students commit suicide at about half the rate of young adults who are not attending college. Reasons for the difference may include limited access to firearms in collegiate settings; stronger family support networks among college-attending youth; greater involvement by pre-college and college students in clubs and sports; greater access to antidepressant medications; and the increased availability of peer, academic, and professional counseling.

Data about completed suicides should not be confused with rates of depression and *contemplated* suicide among college students. Some observers see a significant increase in rates of depression (nearly one in two students becoming "severely depressed" during their undergraduate years) with about 10 percent of college students reporting that they had "seriously considered" suicide.

[2] What should Resident Advisors do when they learn about a suicide threat or attempt?

The cardinal rule when you hear about any threatened or attempted suicide is to seek *professional help immediately*. Suicide is often associated with clinical depression, accompanied by evasion and denial. Don't ask friends or roommates to "watch" a potential victim. Don't accept a student's assertion that a suicide threat was a joke, a "gesture," or the result of a "bad day." *Seek professional help immediately.*

Consider the following advice from psychiatrist Sam Klagsbrun, given in an interview in *Synthesis: Law and Policy in Higher Education:*

"**Synthesis:** How seriously should suicide attempts and threats be taken? Is there any danger that we'll overreact?"

"**Klagsbrun:** The sin of overreacting is a wonderful one to commit. Because what it shows is the availability of the system to react. And if the worst thing that happens is that someone says, 'you're really overreacting, get out of my life,' and pushes you away, then that's the worst that happens. We at least gave the student an option of pushing us away, as opposed to not being cared for by the surrounding community, which is what most people experience."

[3] Is there a connection between suicide and mental illness?

Generally, yes. Psychiatry professor Kay Redfield Jamison at Johns Hopkins University has written that "[t]he overwhelming majority of suicides are linked to psychiatric illnesses," especially clinical depression (*Night Falls Fast*, 1999, p. 81). Given the strong association between suicide and mental illness, suicide training should stress the need for prompt professional intervention. Gatekeepers (like resident advisors) should not regard attempted suicide or serious suicide threats simply as evidence of temporary frustration or exhaustion. It is increasingly apparent that the main obstacle to suicide prevention is *under* reaction, including the failure to hospitalize students and to assist them with appropriate medication.

A pertinent case study on student suicide can be seen at: http://www.collegepubs.com/ref/Suicide_Prevention.shtml

[4] Can more personal connection and attention reduce suicide rates?

The causes of suicide are complex and variable. In general, suicide is often associated with clinical depression. Depression, in turn, can be exacerbated by environmental factors like social isolation. The importance of personal connection and reducing depression was explored in a February 2000 article by author Tim Parks in the *New York Review of Books*. Parks told the story of a mental patient ("Robert," as described by Jay Neugeboren in his book *Imagining Robert: My Brother,*

Madness, and Survival, 1998), who seemed to be making a strong recovery using a new drug:

> Encouraged by this progress, Robert's social worker concentrates on preparing him for the move to the open ward and relative freedom. Everything seems set for at least partial recovery. But two weeks before that crucial move is due, the social worker is abruptly transferred. Despite continuing with [the drug] Robert rapidly deteriorates ... Question ... If the drug works, why does it appear to stop working on the departure of the social worker?

A remarkable answer, Parks suggests, is that various forms of therapy (including the help and attention of a caring staff member) influence the structure of the brain. "[W]hile the brain is indeed conditioned by genetic factors," Parks writes, "it also responds and changes according to environment and experience, the latter often being crucial in the triggering and even transformation of particular genes."

The plasticity of the brain has important implications for medical professionals. Parks wrote that:

> Leston Havens, Professor of Psychiatry at Harvard, [remarked] that despite their reputation for vanity, many mental health professionals, and medical students in particular, fail to recognize their own importance. They 'come and go among patients as if their knowledge and skills were all that counted, their persons not at all ...' [But] [b]y suggesting that the self, patient's and doctor's, is constantly both product and producer of a group dynamic [is] to imply ... that in the long run a patient may respond as much to a 'good morning' as to a drug ...'

Substitute the word "students" for "patients" and the expression "[t]hey 'come and go among patients as if their knowledge and skills were all that counted, their persons not at all ...'" could apply with equal force to resident advisors.

Bottom line: One of the most important things you can do for your residents is to get to know them as individuals. Pay attention to them. Greet them. Listen to their concerns. Develop group activities designed to help students form connections with others, including faculty mentors. Pay attention to "loners" or students who seem left out. Enhanced personal connection is not a panacea for preventing suicide, but it should be an essential component of any suicide prevention program.

[5] What kind of suicide prevention programming should I consider?

Consult with staff members in the health and counseling centers about specific suicide prevention programs they might offer. An additional way of approaching the topic is to sponsor programs about stress reduction, making sure students hear the message that it's a sign of intelligence and maturity to seek professional help if they feel overwhelmed. Students also need to know about the signs of depression, and effective approaches available to treat it.

[6] Can suicide be predicted?

Generally, no. A definitive statement on suicide prediction and prevention was issued by the American Psychiatric Association (APA) in 2003 ("Practice Guideline for the Assessment and Treatment of Patients With Suicidal Behaviors") A review of the APA Practice Guideline (Guideline) in the July 2004 issue of *Psychiatric Times* reported that:

> Suicidal ideation occurs in about 5.6% of the U.S. population, with about 0.7% of the population attempting suicide. The incidence of completed suicide is far lower, at 0.01%. "This rarity of suicide, even in groups known to be at higher risk than the general population, contributes to the impossibility of predicting suicide," according to the [G]uideline.

One factor limiting the effectiveness of suicide prediction is the impulsive nature of most suicides. Kay Redfield Jamison has written that:

> [W]e know that suicidal acts are often impulsive; that is they are undertaken without much forethought or regard for consequence. More than half of suicide attempts occur in a context of a premeditation period of less than five minutes.

[7] Can suicide "risk factors" be identified?

Yes. The inability to predict suicide has not prevented mental health professionals from trying to identify *risk factors* for suicide. Four risk factors cited by The Jed Foundation ("a nonprofit public charity committed to reducing the youth suicide rate") are:

- "Mental Illness: 90% of adolescent suicide victims have at least one diagnosable, active psychiatric illness at the time of death—most often depression, substance abuse, and conduct disorders. Only 15% of suicide victims were in treatment at the time of death."
- "Previous Attempts: 26-33% of adolescent suicide victims have made a previous suicide attempt."
- "Stressors: Suicide in youth often occurs after the victim has gotten into some sort of trouble or has experienced a recent disappointment or rejection."
- "Firearms: Having a firearm in the home greatly increases the risk of youth suicide. 64% of suicide victims 10-24 years old use a firearm to complete the act."

Other frequently cited risk factors include:

- A family history of suicide;
- Recent suicide of a close friend or relation;

- Social stresses associated with being gay or bisexual;
- Legal problems or disciplinary incidents;
- Physical or sexual abuse in childhood;
- Persistent anxiety or panic attacks;
- Demonstrated high levels of aggression and impulsiveness;
- "Lovesickness" or emotional turmoil associated with intimate partner problems.

Individual risk factors can be exacerbated by general environmental conditions, especially seasonality (peak months for suicide are late spring and summer) and dramatic or romanticized publicity about recent suicides.

[8] Should "risk assessment" scores be used to remove students from the residence halls?

No. The APA document "Assessing and Treating Suicidal Behaviors: A Quick Reference Guide" cautions that:

> [S]uicide assessment scales have very low predictive values and do not provide reliable estimates of suicide risk. Nonetheless, they may be useful in developing a thorough line of questioning about suicide or in opening communication with the patient.

Suicide risk assessment protocols used by mental health professionals are not designed to serve the administrative purpose of screening out potentially suicidal students. Guidelines and questions that might be helpful in "opening communication" with students and establishing baseline therapeutic responses (subject to review and modification during the course of counseling and treatment) do not have sufficient predictive value to dismiss students deemed to be "at risk" of suicide. Administrative decisions of that nature are better grounded on demonstrable behavior (e.g. overt suicide threats or attempts), not "predictions" or "risk assessments" about what a student might do in the future.

[9] Are colleges liable when a student suicide occurs?

Liability risks for suicide remain low, at least outside custodial settings where a "special relationship" is likely to arise (e.g. hospitals or inpatient facilities) or when the suicide is "caused" by a defendant (for example, by "illegal and careless" dissemination of drugs) or when a mental health professional fails to meet established standards of diagnosis or care. Current law in the higher education setting was summarized by the Supreme Court of Iowa in *Jain v. State of Iowa* (2000), when it held that knowledge by university officials of a prior suicide attempt in the residence halls by an 18 year old freshman (Sanjay Jain) did not create a "special relationship" giving rise to "an affirmative duty of care." The Jain court observed that "[i]n Iowa and elsewhere, it is the general rule that ... the act of suicide is considered a deliberate, intentional and intervening act that precludes another's responsibility for the harm."

The issue of liability for student suicide in the college and university setting is in flux. While established legal precedent clearly limits the risk, signs of change are on the horizon, intensified by growing activism among parents on the issue of campus safety and security. There is no indication courts or legislatures will impose a requirement that colleges randomly screen and predict which students will commit suicide and make timely interventions to save their lives. Nor will administrators or counselors (who are not mental health professionals) be expected to know and respond to all of the evolving and frequently ambiguous "warning signs" of suicide. Instead, institutions of higher education face heightened risk of liability for suicide when they ignore or mishandle *known suicide threats or attempts*. The immediate practical lesson for resident advisors is to refrain from treating suicide threats or attempts as temporary episodes of depression or disorientation, likely to "go away" on their own. Remember the cardinal rule: When you hear about any threatened or attempted suicide *seek professional help immediately*.

[10] Could liability risks be reduced by dismissing students at risk of suicide?

No. One of the worst things a college or university could do as a "risk management" measure is routinely dismiss students at risk of suicide. Not only would such a practice be ethically questionable, it might also violate the Americans with Disabilities Act, thereby producing *more* litigation. The right educational policy—and the right risk management practice—is to make sure students who threaten or attempt suicide obtain immediate professional help (even if an assessment has to be required, or enforced through the college disciplinary process) and that they remain in school.

[11] Are there any model suicide prevention programs?

The University of Illinois has developed what many observers regard as a model suicide prevention program. Paul Joffe, director of the University of Illinois suicide-prevention program, and a counselor in the University Counseling Center, described the Illinois approach in "The Illinois Plan, Part II," *Synfax Weekly Report* (November, 2003):

> For the last 18 years, the University of Illinois has held its students to a standard of self-welfare and mandated all students who have threatened or attempted suicide to attend four sessions of professional assessment. The most appropriate evidence, which compares the rate of suicide at locations within Champaign County between the eight year pre-program study period with the 18 years

of the program, showed a 55.4 percent reduction in the rate of suicide. To rule out the possibility that this decrease was part of a larger decrease in the rate of suicide, either nationally or at mid-western universities, these results were compared with suicide rates both nationally and at 11 peer institutions in the Big Ten. Both comparisons showed that the rate of suicide at the University of Illinois was declining at that same time rates nationally and within the Big Ten were essentially stable . . .

Of all the myriad risk factors identified to date, none comes close to matching the expression of prior suicidal intent either in predictive power or in potential for leverage. The present program shows that focusing precisely and relentlessly on this single risk factor and creating an elaborate system of reporting and mandated intervention, the rate of suicide can be cut in half.

[12] Should parents be notified when a student threatens or attempts suicide?

Parental notification polices differ. Resident advisors should not contact parents unless directed to do so by a supervisor. Also, in some cases, a mental health professional will advise against parental notification.

As a general rule, parents or other persons identified by students as "emergency contacts" should be notified by designated staff members in cases of threatened or attempted suicide. Experience has shown that families usually come together in a crisis, and that parents see their students holistically in ways college and university staff members are likely to miss. A resident advisor might know a student for a few months. That's no substitute for the knowledge, insight, and devotion of the student's parents. Likewise, it's unwise for college officials to make quick and superficial judgments based on limited evidence that any particular family is "dysfunctional." Families aren't perfect, but neither are college administrators, and (in terms of what a student is truly thinking and feeling) they usually know less than a student's parents.

Consider the following observation from Paul R. McHugh, former chairman of the department of psychiatry at Johns Hopkins School of Medicine (cited in the article "Parents were the last to know" by columnist Eileen McNamara in the January 30, 2002 *Boston Globe*):

Privacy isn't everything; life is everything. We lock people up, we take their civil liberties away if they are a danger to themselves. But we can't call the parents? What kind of nonsense is that?

[13] Where can I go for additional information?

The first place to go for guidance on the subject of college student suicide is your own counseling center. You can also find general advice at this website: http://www.jedfoundation.org/

To learn more about clinical depression (and the feelings of those who experience it) read Kay Redfield Jamison's book *An Unquiet Mind* (Vintage, 1995).

Dr. Jamison also explores the connection between depression and higher levels of personal insight and creativity. Sometimes our best and brightest students will experience sharp swings in moods. It's not our aim to make them "normal" or "conventional" (and certainly not to dismiss them from school), but to help them understand, adjust, and manage their emotions in ways that allow them to achieve their highest potential. Mental health professionals are trained to seek this result, usually through a process that combines carefully dosed medication and some form of cognitive therapy.

Summary and Overview

[a] suicide threats or attempts should be treated as medical emergencies. Seek professional help immediately.

[b] Pay attention to your residents. Be a good listener. Develop group activities designed to help students form connections with others, including faculty mentors.

[c] Sponsor programs about stress reduction and signs of severe depression. Make sure students hear the message that it's a sign of intelligence and maturity to seek professional help.

[d] Suicide is often impulsive. Assisting students in obtaining professional help (especially during a personal crisis) can allow them to acquire resources, insights and skills that sharply lessen the risk of suicide later.

[e] Suicide cannot be predicted, but "risk factors" for suicide can be identified. Risk factor scores should be used by mental health professionals for treatment, not by college officials for administrative action (e.g. a "mandatory medical withdrawal").

[f] Approaches to college student suicide should not be driven by liability concerns. The right educational policy and the right risk management practice is to make sure students who threaten or attempt suicide obtain immediate professional help, even if an assessment has to be required, or enforced through the college disciplinary process.

[g] In most cases of threatened or attempted suicide, parents or other persons identified by students as "emergency contacts" should be notified. Such notification, however, should only be done after consultation with and authorization by your supervisor.

[h] Sometimes the best and brightest students will experience sharp swings in moods. It's not our aim to make them "normal" or "conventional" (and certainly not to dismiss them from school), but to help them understand, adjust, and manage their emotions in ways that allow them to achieve their highest potential.

Appendix E

The Illinois Plan
An empirically supported program to prevent college student suicide

By Paul Joffe*

> *What follows are extended excerpts from commentary about the Illinois plan for suicide prevention, written by Paul Joffe, director of Illinois' suicide-prevention program and a counselor in the University Counseling Center* (p-joffe@ad.uiuc.edu). *The commentary was first delivered at the 2003 Stetson College of Law Annual National Conference on Law and Higher Education and published in 2003 issues of* Synfax Weekly Report *and the* ASJA Law and Policy Report.

[Overview]

"In the fall of 1984, the University of Illinois instituted a formal program to reduce the rate of suicide among its enrolled students. At the core of the program was a policy that required any student who threatened or attempted suicide to attend four sessions of professional assessment. The consequences for failing to comply with the program included withdrawal from the university. In the 19 full years that the program has been in effect, reports on 1670 suicide incidents have been submitted to the Suicide Prevention Team. The rate of suicide at locations within Champaign County decreased from a rate of 6.91 per 100,000 enrolled students during the eight years before the program started to a rate of 2.90 during the 19 years of the program. This represents a reduction of 58.0 percent. This reduction occurred against a backdrop of stable rates of suicide both nationally and among 11 peer institutions within the Big Ten."

[Extent of college student suicide]

"After decades of debate over whether the rate of suicide was higher or lower among college-attending young adults, Schwartz and

---

**Full text of the Joffe article with citations is available at: http://jedfoundation.org/ articles/joffeuniversityofillinoisprogram.pdf

Reifler (1980), Bessai (1986), Schwartz and Reifler (1988), Schwartz and Whitaker (1990), and Silverman, Meyer, Sloane, Raffel and Pratt (1997), convincingly established the rate to be roughly half the rate for young adults in the general population. While the number of students who kill themselves on any given campus in any given year is thankfully small, extrapolating from the 14.9 million students enrolled in 2001, approximately 1100 young adults kill themselves in the nation's colleges and universities every year . . ."

[Colleges are "mired in inaction"]

"[D]espite the death of 1100 students a year, institutions of higher education have been the scene of surprisingly few systematic efforts to lower the rate of suicide. In the sixty-five years since Rapheal, Power and Berridge (1937) published the first study of college suicide at the University of Michigan, the majority of published papers have detailed the demographic and psychological profiles of students who have committed suicide . . . While several writers have made specific recommendations, there have been only two formal proposals for systematic efforts to prevent suicide (Webb, 1986; Westefeld & Pattillo, 1986).

"There have been only six reports of systematic programs (Dashef, 1984; Ottens, 1984; Funderburk & Archer 1989; Whitaker & Slimak, 1990; Meilman, Pattis & Kraus-Zeilmann, 1994; Jed Foundation, 2001). These six programs have either been short-lived or not associated with empirical evidence that would allow an evaluation of their effectiveness. Instead of leading the nation in suicide prevention, colleges and universities are mired in inaction. While renowned for their leadership in other fields, to this day there has not been a single campus-based effort to prevent suicide that has solid empirical evidence to support its practice."

[Four categories of programs]

"Campus prevention projects, both proposed and undertaken, can be divided into one of four overlapping categories, 1) cultivation of a community of caring, 2) identification and referral of at-risk students, 3) reduction of academic stress, and 4) postvention following a completed suicide. Proponents of a community of caring approach include Knott (1973), Benard and Benard (1980), Webb (1986), Whitaker (1986) and Whitaker and Slimak (1990). Undoubtedly the most comprehensive implementation of the community of caring approach was the University of Florida's Suicide Prevention Project.

"The project focused on educating the university community around the problems of stress, self-destructive behaviors and suicide. It included a newsletter, public service announcements and advertisements in an effort to reduce stress, encourage psychological balance and challenge the campus community to be more supportive of one another. Also known as 'The Campus Cares,' the Suicide Prevention Project began in 1986 and continued for 10 years until 1995. Unfortunately, there was no effort to gather empirical evidence on its impact on the university's rate of suicide.

"The second type of suicide prevention effort has been to lesson barriers to professional treatment and increase the likelihood that depressed and suicidal students will receive appropriate assistance. After four suicides in 1977-78, Cornell University launched a program to train 50 students, staff and faculty a year in crisis intervention and referral (Ottens, 1984). Dashef (1984) reported on a multi-faceted project at the University of Massachusetts at Amherst. It included educational outreach around warning signs and referral procedures, an expansion of treatment resources, closer collaboration with community hospitals and a hands-on approach to intervention. Dashef reports that six students committed suicide in the year prior to the program and following its implementation, there was a period of 15 months without a suicide.

"The College of William and Mary, with an enrollment of 7,500 students, fortified the referral process by requiring students at risk of committing suicide to participate in an immediate professional evaluation (Meilman et al., 1994). Meilman et al. (1994) reported that only two students committed suicide during a 25 year period. The Jed Foundation (2001), a nonprofit public charity committed to reducing the rate of suicide among young adults, has been working with institutions of higher education to take a comprehensive look at their mental health services and suicide prevention efforts to insure they meet essential standards. Simultaneously, the Jed Foundation has developed a web-based screening instrument that allows students to assess themselves and be connected directly with campus professionals. At present, the web service is available to over 400,000 students at 28 colleges and universities.

"The third approach to suicide prevention has been to reduce the stressors, particularly academic, that might predispose a student to commit suicide. Knott (1973) called for a lessening of competitive pressures. Perhaps the most comprehensive approach has been proposed by the Jed Foundation. Among its recommendations is a more student-friendly medical leave policy.

"The fourth category of prevention effort has been to work with the survivors of completed suicides (Benard & Benard, 1980). Perhaps the most articulate proponent of 'postvention' has been Webb (1986). Citing research that has found that the death by suicide of a family member is a risk factor for the surviving members of the family, Webb reasoned that the college friends of a student who committed suicide would also be at greater risk. By providing the campus community with a range of bereavement services, Webb proposed this risk could be reduced."

[Little evidence of beneficial impact]

"One might conclude that with the except for Dashef (1984), the Jed Foundation (2001), and in particular Meilman et al. (1994), that proposals and projects to reduce the rate of college suicide have been more well-meaning than meaningfully effective. While few would argue against the importance of a compassionate and caring environment, it becomes difficult to see caring alone as the keystone of any systematic intervention.

"With the exception of Meilman et al. (1994), efforts to identity and refer suicidal students are based on the assumption that such students would be willing to participate in treatment or at best demonstrate mild resistance. No author has drawn a distinction between the resistance to treatment shown in the general population and the outright rejection of treatment shown by the majority of suicidal individuals.

"Efforts to reduce academic stress would seem to overlook conflicting evidence regarding its role in college suicide. Benard and Benard (1982) reported that among 75 undergraduates enrolled at Memphis State who reported making threats or attempts while in college, 52 percent gave social problems as the reason, 21 percent gave family problems and only 7 percent gave academic pressures. Meilman et al. (1994) reported that among 11 students at William and Mary who attempted suicide in 1991, 91⁄ had evidence of work or school failure, while 46 percent had evidence of relationship difficulties or breakups. Among 14 students at William [and Mary] who threatened suicide, 36 percent had evidence of work or school failure and 64 percent had evidence of relationship difficulties or breakups. And finally, while suicide postvention is a critical service in its own right, there is no evidence to support the contention that peer survivors of college suicide are associated with an increased risk of suicide themselves."

[Analysis of suicide risk factors]

"The enterprise of preventing suicide is largely one of identifying risk factors and translating them into effective interventions. Ross (1969) identified 21 separate risk factors associated with an increased risk of suicide among college students, including depression, death of one's father, and lack of close personal relationships. Benard and Benard (1985) identified 37 and Slimak (1990) identified 41. Despite the steadily increasing number of known risk factors, there has not been a corresponding increase in the number or intensity of prevention efforts.

"Of all the risk factors that have been identified, none have been more thoroughly researched than the presence of prior suicidal intent. Most often, researchers have set the threshold for prior intent as the presence of a suicide attempt serious enough to result in a stay at an inpatient psychiatric hospital (see Maris, 1992 for a review). Other researchers have set the threshold at a suicide attempt that required medical attention in an emergency room. Dorpat and Riley (1967), in a review of the literature, concluded that between 40 and 65 percent of individuals who committed suicide gave unmistakable evidence of prior intent based on the occurrence of a serious prior suicide attempt. When researchers have used more inclusive measures of prior suicidal intent, this figure becomes considerably higher ..."

[A statement of suicidal intent is an "action"]

"Not only is the presence of demonstrated suicidal intent the single most powerful predictor of eventual suicide, it stands apart from all other risk factors in that it is an 'action.' As an action it can be subject to a code of conduct and administrative sanction. All other risk factors—depression, social isolation, loss of a parent in adolescence, or a family member who committed suicide—are 'statuses.' Statuses, whether psychological, social, or historical, cannot be subject to administrative leverage."

[Most suicidal individuals won't be seen by health and counseling centers]

"A number of researchers have noted that contrary to expectations, only a small percentage of students who commit suicide have had prior contact with campus mental health personnel. Braaten and Darling (1962) reported that the students who recently committed suicide at Cornell University were not patients at the university's mental health services. Schwartz and Whittaker (1990) conducted a meta-analysis of four studies that reported rates of prior professional contact and found that among 99 students who committed suicide, only 36 had such contact.

"These findings are consistent with studies of suicide among nonstudent populations ... Moeller (1989) noted that research on the effectiveness of post-attempt aftercare is made difficult by the inherently low rate of treatment compliance. Hoffman (2000) citing these statistics suggested that most suicide prevention centers and the traditional provision of mental health resources will 'miss' the majority of individuals most at risk."

[Suicidal intent and student belief structures]

"Eighteen years of working intensively with suicidal students at the University of Illinois has led to a number of counterintuitive observations. Suicidal intent, the driving force behind suicidal action, does not exist in a vacuum. Instead, it is often accompanied by other deeply held beliefs and entrenched character structures. According to the widely held distress model of suicide, popularized by the interpretation that suicidal behavior is a 'cry for help,' no individual would want to be suicidal and that any student who had the misfortune of being saddled with suicidal intent, would gladly forfeit it at the first opportunity.

"It would surprise campus administrators to know that while suicidal students might or might not feel distressed about conditions in their lives, they generally don't feel distressed about being suicidal. Many will openly admit that being suicidal is one of the few, if not the only, bright spots in their lives. Instead of seeing suicide as a problem, they see it as a solution to their problems. Many are proud, if not proudly defiant, of their power to control their own fate, many are identified with and attached to their capacity for self-destruction, and the majority will resist with considerable tenacity any proposal that they give it up (See Caruso, 1986, for example). As long as campus prevention efforts overlook the darker co-companions of being in college and being suicidal, such students will remain tragically out of reach traditionally configured mental health services.

"Suicidal intent is less a natural response to distress and more the expression of a virulent ideology. It is less founded in desperation and more in control. One cannot simply 'refer' suicidal students because they will not accept such referrals. In the unlikely event that he "accepts" a referral, it is unlikely he will either make the appointment or keep it. In the unlikely event he keeps the first appointment, he is unlikely to raise the threat or attempt, and instead minimize it or regard it as ancient history. In the highly unlikely event that he keeps a second appointment, it is unlikely that he will tolerate an open discussion of the incident or its implications.

"The likelihood of a student voluntarily engaging in a meaningful assessment of the incident and its implications across four appointments is estimated at less than five percent. If the elements of a meaningful intervention are to be present in contacts with mental health professionals, they must be imported administratively. Attempts to refer through traditional means the students most at risk—students who have advertised their intent by making threats and attempts—is currently the weak link of campus prevention efforts.

"The ineffectiveness of referring students after a suicide threat or attempt is only half the problem. The other half is the response of the mental health professionals to the suicidal students in their midst. Most college campuses lack a standard-of-response following a threat or attempt. Quite often, it is psychiatrists, working out of a medical model, who triage the emergency response to suicidal incidents. A referral for therapy is often only made if the student requests it, which is surprisingly seldom. Mental health professionals often try to sort out students who are truly serious about suicide from those who are not serious, despite research that questions the predictive value of such judgments.

"If a suicidal student does meet with a social worker or psychologist, more often than not, that contact is brief. The therapist typically lacks an independent source of information regarding the incident. Instead of having the suicide note, police report or emergency room summary in his or her possession, the therapist is forced to rely on the student's reconstruction, which usually places the best face on the event. The decision of whether to continue meeting with this student is completely at the therapist's discretion. Given enormous demands from students who want to be seen for counseling and the recently suicidal student who generally does not want such services, the therapist will often agree with the student to end treatment prematurely."

[A research base]

"The University of Illinois is a large land-grant institution located 140 miles south of Chicago in the center of a large rural county with a population of 179,699 as reported in the 2000 Census. In the fall of 2001 there were 37,684 enrolled students. Of these, 28,114 were undergraduates enrolled in 150 degree programs and 9,570 were graduate and professional students enrolled in over 100 fields of study. Fifty-three percent were male and forty-seven percent female. The university has a strong international presence with 4,283 students representing 119 different countries. Ninety percent of the undergraduates were Illinois residents, with the vast majority coming from Chicago and its surrounding suburbs. University residence halls provide accommodations for 9,200 students with the remaining living off campus in 52 fraternities, 29 sororities, and a variety of apartments and houses.

"In 1983, the Counseling Center contracted with the Champaign County Coroner's Office to examine its records and provide the Center with the names and psychoautopsies of all students who committed suicide within Champaign County between academic years 1976 and 1983. Their names were submitted to the Office of the Registrar which provided transcripts to verify that they had been enrolled at the university at the time of their death or had been enrolled at some point six months prior to their death. Nineteen students met these criteria. Of these nineteen students, 16 were male, 3 female; 16 were undergraduates, 3 were graduate or professional students. The incidence of suicide was determined to be 6.91 students per 100,000 enrolled students. This compared favorably with a rate of 12.5 per 100,000 among 15-24 year-olds in the general population.

"In addition to the 19 enrolled students who committed suicide within Champaign County, it was assumed that there were additional students who committed suicide at locations outside of the county, principally at their family-of-origin residence over weekends and breaks. Attempts to retrospectively obtain the names of students who committed suicide outside of Champaign County from deans, mental health professionals and university administrators proved unsuccessful. The difficulty of determining with sufficient certainty away-from-campus suicides has been cited as a conundrum in accurately establishing the rate of suicide in higher education (Benard & Benard, 1985; Silverman et al. 1997).

"Of particular interest in the pre-program coroner study was the pattern of mental health usage among students who eventually committed suicide. A major finding was the disproportionate contact they had with various disciplines of the mental health profession. Thirteen of the students or 68 percent were in treatment with either a university or community psychiatrist. One student or five percent was identified as having had appointments with a clinical psychologist. Of additional interest was the extent to which the Coroner's Office, in their limited investigation, found evidence of previous threats and attempts. Twelve of the 19 students or 63 percent had given tangible indications of their suicidal intent in the form of a public threat or attempt."

[Starting the program with "invite and encourage"]

"Based on the coroner's findings, the Counseling Center established the Suicide Prevention Program, the purpose of which was to undertake activities that might lead to a reduction in the rate of suicide. The initial focus of the program's efforts was to restrict access to lethal means of committing suicide, in particular laboratory cyanide, the means of death in three of the 19 suicides. The second project was to increase the percentage of students meeting with social workers and psychologists following a suicide threat or attempt. The reasons for the low rate of contact was still a mystery and the members of the program started with the assumption that students either were not being referred or were unaware that such services existed free-of-charge. The initial program could be best described as one of 'invite and encourage.' The Suicide Prevention Team mobilized residence hall staff, friends, mental health professionals, deans, faculty and other administrators to make direct contact with students in the week after a threat or attempt and invite and encourage them to make one or more appointments with a therapist for the purposes of exploring the roots of their suicidal intent.

"The project of invite and encourage lasted for three months and the results were wholly unsuccessful in increasing the number of contacts with social workers and psychologists. The project was successful, however, in providing the members of the program with direct contact with students who recently threatened and attempted suicide and a number of curious phenomena were noticed. A surprising number of students emphatically denied that they had ever made a suicide threat or attempt in spite of the existence of suicide notes, eyewitnesses and other evidence to the contrary. A large number of students admitted to having been suicidal at the time of the incident but claimed to have made a complete and lasting recovery, making meeting with a social worker or psychologist unnecessary.

"A number of students would acquiesce to the request to make an appointment but not actually make it. Some students would schedule an appointment but not keep it. Several students attended appointments but did not inform the therapist of the recent attempt and instead focused on career issues or a problem with procrastination. A few students lied, telling their residence hall director that they were meeting with a professional when they were not. A few students met with professionals once but failed to keep a second or a third appointment. Another common phenomena was complete disappearance—students would not answer phone calls or respond to visits and literally could not be found for weeks. Despite the combined efforts of a cast of dozens, it was estimated that less than five percent of students contacted, met with a social worker or psychologist for four times."

[Moving to "mandated assessment"]

"In October, 1984 the program of invite and encourage was abandoned and in its place an administrative policy was crafted as an extension of the psychiatric withdrawal policy. The new policy mandated any student who made a suicide threat or attempt to receive four sessions of professional assessment. The first appointment was to occur within a week of the incident or release from the hospital and the remaining sessions would ideally occur at weekly intervals. Failure to comply with the mandate could result in a variety of sanctions, including academic encumbrance, disciplinary suspension and/or involuntary psychiatric withdrawal.

"The program of mandated assessment addressed a shortcoming that exists with the prevailing standard-of-response that relies exclusively on the presence of imminent risk of harm to self. The leverage afforded the community when the threshold of imminent risk has been reached is well developed at colleges and universities. Unfortunately, only a small percentage of students displaying suicidal intent reach this threshold. Also the leverage afforded by imminent risk persists for only the short period of time immediately surrounding the suicidal crisis and vanishes as soon as it is over.

"The Suicide Prevention Program drew a distinction between imminent and proximal risk. Imminent risk refers to risk posed by current suicidal intent associated with ready access to means of self-harm.

Proximal risk refers to the increased risk of suicide associated with displays of a wide range of suicidal intent in the year following that display. It was estimated that a student who threatened or attempted suicide was 543 times more likely to commit suicide in the following year than his or her roommates or classmates who had not threatened or attempted. The Suicide Prevention Program addressed proximal risk by providing leverage for intervention in the months that followed a display of suicidal intent."

[Creating a prevention team]

"A Suicide Prevention Team was created to administer the policy. The Team consisted of four members: Two psychologists, a social worker and an administrative specialist. Two of the professionals worked at the Counseling Center, the third worked at the mental health department associated with the university health center. The Team met every other week for 30 to 60 minutes, largely to review compliance. The members of the Team remained in close contact between meetings by phone and e-mail.

"Licensed social workers and psychologists constituted eligible assessors. Meetings with psychiatrists were encouraged but did not count towards the requirement if the focus of the session was medication assessment. Students had the option of satisfying the requirement by meeting with private therapists in the community but only at their own expense and only after signing a release authorizing the Team to debrief the therapist on the suicidal incident and to monitor compliance . . .

"Over the 18 years of the program has been effect, the Suicide Prevention Team evolved into a quasi-conduct and discipline office. Its authority flowed from the Office of Dean of Students. It adjudicated a single standard of conduct regarding self-welfare and it recommended a limited scope of sanctions to the Dean. The Team adjudicated the threshold of action necessary to trigger a valid report. It adjudicated what constituted suicidal intent. It adjudicated disputes over what manner of professional contact counted towards satisfying the four session requirement. Because of the strict demands for confidentiality, the Team was comprised solely of mental health professionals."

[Required "suicide incident report form"]

"The Suicide Prevention Program benefited from a 1977 memo from the Vice Chancellor for Student Affairs that required all Student Affairs staff to submit a Suicide Incident Report Form (SIRF) to the Counseling Center whenever they had credible information that a student had threatened or attempted suicide. Faculty and other staff members were invited to report but not required. The SIRF was not a current assessment of suicidal risk. Instead, it documented retrospectively that a given student crossed the line from passing thoughts of suicide to concrete and observable actions. Qualifying actions included preparation of means (e.g. purchasing pills), practicing of means (e.g. holding a knife over one's wrist), public statements, and attempts. The duration of these actions might be measured in seconds, e.g. putting pills in one's mouth and immediately spitting them out, and still constitute a crossing of the threshold.

"Reports were to be submitted for incidents that had occurred up to three months previously. Once this threshold had been crossed, no other distinctions were made. The same report and resulting mandate would apply to a student who took three Tylenol (with the intent of dying), a student who took 100 Tylenol, or the student who bought 100 Tylenol for the purposes of killing herself but did not actually take them. No distinction was made between those who clearly wanted to die and those who appeared to want the attention of others or appeared to want to exercise leverage over another person. The program sidestepped the second-guessing that is common among professionals regarding the meaning and seriousness of self-destructive acts. The program's philosophy was that anyone who had crossed the threshold from passing thoughts to taking action was at increased risk for eventual suicide."

[What mandated assessment entails]

"The program was termed 'mandated assessment' as opposed to 'mandated therapy' because of the perspective that one cannot mandate treatment. In this context of assessment the professional, at a minimum, would assess the student's current ideation, intent and access to means. Second, the professional would work with the student to reconstruct the circumstances, thoughts and feelings that surrounded and precipitated the original incident. Third, the professional would take a lifetime history of the student's suicidal intent and its various meanings and origins. Fourth, the professional would draw attention to the university's standard of self-welfare and the consequences for failing to adhere to it. These four issues would be addressed during each of the four sessions. Once addressed, the professional and student would be free to use the remaining time to explore issues that might have contributed to the threat or attempt and barring these, any issue of the student's choosing. The overwhelming majority of students made full use of the allotted time ...

"While the requirement of four professional sessions was the most obvious feature of the prevention program, the requirement was only the front line of a multi-layered response. At each step of the program, the student was assessed for his or her ability and willingness to adhere to the standard of self-welfare ... In especially entrenched cases involving alcohol abuse, open defiance, or fast-moving developments, special teams were convened to fashion the best response. The program adapted to the student, meeting an inability or unwillingness to adhere to the standard with increasing firmness ..."

[Program results]

"For the last 18 years, the University of Illinois has held its students to a standard of self-welfare and mandated all students who have threatened or attempted suicide to attend four sessions of professional assessment. The most appropriate evidence, which compares the rate of suicide at locations within Champaign County between the eight year pre-program study period with the 18 years of the program, showed a 55.4 percent reduction in the rate of suicide. To rule out the possibility that this decrease was part of a larger decrease in the rate of suicide, either nationally or at mid-western universities, these results were compared with suicide rates both nationally and at 11 peer institutions in the Big Ten. Both comparisons showed that the rate of suicide at the University of Illinois was declining at that same time rates nationally and within the Big Ten were essentially stable."

[Conclusion]

"Of all the myriad risk factors identified to date, none comes close to matching the expression of prior suicidal intent either in predictive power or in potential for leverage. The present program shows that focusing precisely and relentlessly on this single risk factor and creating an elaborate system of reporting and mandated intervention, the rate of suicide can be cut in half. Universities are untapped natural laboratories for innovative programs to prevent suicide. Instead of lagging behind, they have the potential to lead the nation, saving not only the lives of their own students but of Americans in general."

"A response to Gary Pavela's question regarding what elements might be responsible for the decline in the rate of suicide associated with the University of Illinois' Suicide Prevention Program"

by Paul Joffe, December 9, 2003

"Preface

"Since it was established in 1984, the Suicide Prevention Program at the University of Illinois at Urbana-Champaign has been associated with a 58 percent decline in the rate of suicide. What's more, the program has been wholly effective in deterring students who have given indication of suicidal intent from committing suicide. Each of the 20 students who committed suicide in the last 19 years has done so 'out of the blue.' In contrast, none of the students detailed in the 1670 suicide incident reports received since 1984 has committed suicide.

"While there is evidence that the program has been effective in deterring those students who give evidence of suicidal intent, the question becomes which precise elements of the program are responsible for its success? Is the essential element the four, one-hour appointments with a professional? Is it the quasi-legal challenge by the campus community? Is it the concern for the student's welfare and the caring shown by the campus?

"While it would be impossible to pin down the precise elements without controlled studies, I would like to suggest two possible pathways."

"Pathway 1:
In order to commit suicide, one must experience oneself
to be 'in-charge' of whether one lives or dies.
The Suicide Prevention Program directly challenges
this in-chargeness by assuming a stance of in-chargeness
over the student's continued enrollment.

"I would propose that a person can exist in one of two competing states of mind. One can either experience oneself to be 'in-charge' of a person, place or thing. Or one can defer to something or someone outside of oneself and experience this external entity to be legitimately in-charge of a person, place or thing.

"When it comes to eating, for example, most of us experience ourselves to be in-charge of a series of nested domains, starting with choosing what to eat, obtaining the chosen food, putting the food into our mouths, chewing the food, and finally, swallowing it. But once the swallowed food passes through the esophagus and settles in the stomach, it is 'out of our hands.' It is now in the hands of our stomach and we defer completely to our stomach to subject the swallowed food to its chemical will. If we happen to regret what we have eaten, the expression of that regret is restricted to informing our food choices in the future.

"In contrast, someone who is bulimic has a different profile of in-chargeness. He or she not only experiences himself or herself to be in-charge of the sequence of domains outlined above, but also experiences himself or herself to be the master of his or her stomach. With a finger as a tool, he or she can induce the stomach to vacate its contents and in the process, call a halt to digestion. In further contrast, someone who uses laxatives, experiences himself or herself to be additionally in-charge of his or her intestines. Through the use of a chemical agent, he or she can hold sway over the intestines and block them from absorbing the nutritional content of the swallowed food.

"Our knowledge of bulimia informs us that once a person has assumed charge of a new domain, it can be difficult to give up. As a result of their new-found in-chargeness, a bulimic can experience a sense of power and personal identity. Over time, he or she will likely become attached to being in-charge and resist appeals and attempts to revert back to a state of deferral.

"When it comes to the all important domain of 'personal existence,' most of us adopt the stance of complete deferral. Some of us defer to a higher power to decide when it is time to 'call us home.' Others defer to fate or circumstance and still others surrender themselves to their body's capacity to continue living. In order to even contemplate committing suicide, an individual must first leave the stance of deferral and see themselves as fundamentally in-charge of their continued existence. And mirroring the experiences of those with an eating disorder, those individuals who experience themselves as in-charge of their continued existence for even a short period of time, encounter a rush of power and personal identity.

"Communities are not strangers to individuals in their midst inappropriately assuming a stance of in-chargeness over a given domain. Nor are they strangers to contests over in-chargeness. The criminal justice system (or on campus, the conduct and discipline system) is an institution that specializes in entering into contests with citizens who inappropriately take charge of other peoples' property and decisions.

"Recognizing the critical role that the structures of being in-charge play in the suicidal process, the Suicide Prevention Program attempts to engage these structures within suicidal students with the goal of persuading these students to stand down from their current state of in-chargeness. Experience has shown that the best way to engage these structures is not necessarily through being more warm, more caring or concerned. Instead, the best way to engage these structures in suicidal students is to arouse these same structures within selected university officials and communicate structure to structure.

"To this end, the members of the Suicide Prevention Team are given the authority to negotiate directly with suicidal students over the looming consequences associated with being suicidal. Just as each student is in-charge of whether they live or die, each administrator is in-charge, through the authority of the Dean, of whether the student continues to be enrolled or is withdrawn. The program formally recognizes that the student has assumed a stance of in-chargeness over their continued existence. At the same time, it calls attention to the fact that the administrator is in charge of the continued existence of a valued membership.

"In so many words, the Team member says to the student, 'It is clear from your recent suicide attempt that you currently deem yourself to be in-charge of your continued existence. We are contacting you to inform you that we deem suicidal behavior to be an act of self-directed violence. Given the campus's zero tolerance of violence, your recent behavior is unacceptable. As you may or may not already be aware, the university is in-charge of your continued enrollment as a student. If you persist in being in-charge of your continued existence, I will petition the Dean to exercise his in-chargeness over your continued enrollment and ask him to withdraw you.'*

"The fact that students are subsequently forced to meet with a mental health professional, against their will, and talk about the current status of their in-chargeness, emphasizes that the university can and will constitute itself as an entity in-charge of domains it deems critical . . .

"Because of misconceptions about suicide, namely that suicidal behavior is a cry for help and that suicidal students would otherwise seek appropriate services on their own and because of an insistence that all suicide prevention efforts be steeped in caring and support, campus communities have been reluctant to challenge students at this level. Traditionally, suicidal behavior has been seen as a mental health issue. Clinicians who meet with such students are expected to provide support and assist them in finding reasons to continue living. I would argue that the mental health culture is not nearly as effective at deterring inappropriate in-chargeness as the conduct and discipline culture. In this respect, the Suicide Prevention Program has far more in common with an office of conduct and discipline than with a counseling center."

"Pathway 2:
The Program compensates for an impairment in the mental structures of striving for something more versus striving for something workable.

"I would propose that a person can strive for one of two competing outcomes. An individual can strive for something more, or an individual can strive for something that works. For example, each of us can strive for more money, more closeness, more attention, more approval, more horsepower under the hood, more carats in the ring, more security, or more control. Alternatively, each of us can strive for a workable security, a workable closeness, a workable personal finance, or a workable control.

"These two strivings, for more and for workability, compete with one another and an increase in one inclination leads to a corresponding decrease in the other inclination. For each additional step a person takes towards striv-

---

* "The goal of the Suicide Prevention Program is not to withdraw students—and only one student has been withdrawn in the 19 year history of the program. In that case she was readmitted three months later."

ing for more, there is a corresponding decrease in his or her ability to appreciate the workability of his or her schemes. A person inclined to 'morist' excess might binge-talk, binge-eat, binge-drink, binge-shop and in the context of bingeing, be oblivious to the costs and consequences associated with these actions.

"The more a person strives for more, the less able they are to appreciate reality and the workability or unworkability of their plans. Conversely, the more a person strives to have things work, the more satisfied they become with what they already have and the less likely they are to strive for more.

"A person in the midst of a suicidal career can be expected to be biased if not stuck outright, in an inclination of striving for more. I recently had a conversation with a suicidal student who was simultaneously entertaining 15 separate career possibilities, from teacher to businessman. His life was a mess of tangled additions. But because he was stuck in 'morism,' little, if anything, worked. He had no ability to focus on fundamentals or get back to basics. What he wanted more of, more than anything else, was more power and control. Ultimately, he aspired to be the arbiter of his own life by being in-charge of whether he continued to live or die. Understandably, with little forward traction, he experienced his life as frustrating. But rather than dig in and make things better, he preferred to abandon himself and try his chances with what might lie over the horizon.

"In sharp contrast, a person biased towards striving for workability strives to have any new plan or endeavor work. And in order to truly work, it must work at a number of levels. It must work now and it must work later. It must work for him or her and it must work for other people.

"I would argue that any young adult who is in the midst of a suicidal career has an impairment of this structure of striving for something more versus striving for something that works. Suicide has been described as a 'permanent solution to a temporary problem.' This statement highlights the suicidal student's impaired ability to appreciate the unworkability of their lethal plans. Because death will bring with it undeniable changes in circumstance—feelings will stop, people will be affected—suicide certainly works noticeably in the present. But its benefits cannot be enjoyed in the long run, because the person will not be on hand to appreciate them. Any person who has a reasonably healthy ability to strive for workable solutions, workable control and workable influence, would readily engage in the mental calculations necessary to determine that suicide does not work at several key levels and discard it in favor of more promising options.

"There are many areas in which students engage in morist strivings and as a result, overreach. For example, he or she might tell a joke that is not funny, overstate an opinion that is not supported by the facts, purchase things without sufficient savings, disclose personal details that the current relationship cannot support, drink more than his or her body can tolerate and stay up later and in the process get less sleep than is biologically viable. In each case, after a period of overextending, they will fall flat, sometimes more gently than others, and hopefully think twice before striving similarly for more in the future.

"In effect, a student in a suicidal career is seriously overreaching. His or her scheme of achieving more control will fundamentally not work. Unfortunately, the consequence of this type of overreaching is not merely debt, embarrassment or a hangover, but death.

"The traditional ways that campus communities have responded to students giving evidence of a suicidal career have done little to challenge these students' bias towards "morism" or the underlying impairment that results. Instead, the community's concerned, but hands-off approach, might be confused for neutrality or even romantic approval. But most importantly, the community's response provides no counterweight to the student's morist agenda, no evidence that what the student is striving for will simply not work.

"The Suicide Prevention Program of the University of Illinois strives to provide suicidal students with as much feedback through as many conceivable channels that what they are contemplating will not work. It variously informs them that it will not work for them and it will not work for their community. It will not work now and it will not work in the future. It accomplishes this by a number of specific communications. First, by equating acts of self-harm with acts of violence and suicide with self-murder, the university signals its consistent disapproval. Second, by linking their suicidal behavior directly to their enrollment status, the university is stating that failing to appreciate how their plans will not work at a biological level, that additionally, it will not work at an academic level. Specifically, their suicidal behavior to date has placed them in acute academic jeopardy, as evidenced by forced meetings with a university clinician. They are further informed that future suicidal behavior might well result in the their official separation from the university community. These same simple messages are repeated loudly and consistently.

"It could be the case that the unworkability of suicide at a later date is lost in the hubris of morist excess. Ironically, their current academic jeopardy, coupled with the prospect of being withdrawn in the near future, might be more dear and tangible to them than the prospect of forfeiting their own lives. Death is an abstraction to the suicidal, where expulsion is gut-real. Samuel Johnson once wrote that 'nothing focuses the mind like a sentence of [death].' Apparently this doesn't apply to students ensconced in a suicidal career. Instead, nothing focuses the mind like the prospect of academic withdrawal.

"In some respects, the university serves as a temporary proxy, standing in for suicidal students' impaired ability to accurately calculate the workability of their strivings for more power and control. The university does the math and then translates the results into the single currency that a college student might best understand. Such students, feeling the present sting of academic censure and the future possibility of disenrollment, realize dimly that their current plans are unworkable, quietly abandon them and move on to less lethal waters."

Author's Note:
"Direct threat" analysis and the Illinois mandated assessment policy

How can colleges responsibly undertake "direct threat" analysis given the difficulties involved in predicting future behavior? The answer is to focus on specific conduct that violates reasonable institutional standards, evaluating any threat to self or others in light of proven violations in the past. A suicide threat, for example, is first of all a threat of violence. Threats of violence may be sanctioned through the campus disciplinary system (or an administrative equivalent), after appropriate due process. Any resulting institutional response can be influenced by reasoned assessment of the future risk of violence, including specific statements made by the student respondent; the nature of family and social support systems; and available treatment options. We think this approach is fair and humane to students (including the general population of students who encounter the emotional turmoil of repeated suicide threats or attempts in the residence halls) and is likely to withstand legal scrutiny under federal disabilities law.

Do any such policies exist? A close parallel can be found in the "mandated assessment" policy at the University of Illinois. The Illinois approach is heavily reliant upon the expertise of mental health professionals, but remains grounded in the declaration that "[f]ailure to adhere to [the University's] standard of self-welfare or failure to fulfill the requirements of the assessment following a suicidal incident may result in disciplinary referral ..." Due process is provided in the context of an appeal to the Dean of Students.

The full text of the Illinois policy follows:

"December 10, 2004
Version 6

"Mandated assessment following suicide threats and attempts
"The University of Illinois expects and encourages students to maintain a reasonable concern for their own self-welfare. One of the

times the University formally requires that such a concern be maintained is in the area of suicide.

"In the event that the University is presented with a credible report that a student has threatened or attempted suicide, engaged in efforts to prepare to commit suicide or expressed a preoccupation with suicide, that student will be required to attend four sessions of professional assessment. The purpose of this assessment is to provide the student with resources to adhere to this standard in the future and to monitor the student's willingness and ability to adhere to this standard."

"A. Procedures

"[1] When the Suicide Prevention Team is in receipt of a credible report that a student has threatened or attempted suicide, engaged in efforts to prepare to commit suicide or expressed a preoccupation with suicide, the student will be required to attend four one hour sessions of professional assessment with a licensed mental health professional who agrees to participate in the program's requirement of a comprehensive and in-depth assessment of the precipitating incident, prior attempts and threats, and current suicidal intent. In addition, the professional must be willing and available to engage in counseling and/or therapy, if the student so consents.

"[2] The first assessment will occur within a week of the incident or release from the hospital.

"[3] The remaining assessments will ideally occur at weekly intervals.

"[4] Students are required to participate only in an assessment of their past and current suicidality. Students are not required to engage in counseling or therapy. A student may elect to go beyond the required assessment and participate in counseling or therapy, only after the professional secures the student's permission through verbal consent.

"[5] Students can obtain the assessments with a private practitioner with comparable credentials at his or her own expense and after signing an authorization allowing that practitioner to communicate with members of the Suicide Prevention Team. All professionals will make the incident, its roots and implications a significant focus of each of the four assessments.

"[6] Students seeking to obtain the four assessment appointments with a private practitioner must sign a release allowing the practitioner to make contact with a member of the Suicide Prevention Team. As was the case with university professionals, before meeting with the student, the private practitioner must be provided with independent sources of information regarding the suicidal incident, if such reports exist.

These include suicide notes, police reports, emergency room reports and eye witness accounts.

"[7] Private practitioners will be required, during the period in which the four session assessment occurs, to provide the University with reports of instances in which the student threatened or attempted suicide, engaged in efforts to prepare to commit suicide or expressed a preoccupation with suicide.

"[8] The chair of the Suicide Prevention Team will advise the Dean of Students in the event that a student does not comply with the policy.

"[9] Failure to adhere to this standard of self-welfare or failure to fulfill the requirements of the assessment following a suicidal incident may result in disciplinary referral, academic encumbrance, suspension and/or withdrawal. The appropriate actions associated with this policy will be determined by the Dean of Students.

"[10] The Dean of Students may take other steps, including contacting the student's parents and/or other significant others in the event of a particularly potentially lethal suicide attempt or in the event of repeated suicide attempts."

"B. Confidentiality

"[1] All records associated with the reported incident are kept separately by the Suicide Prevention Team and do not appear as part of the student's academic record.

"[2] All records associated with the mandated assessment are protected by state laws regarding confidentiality."

"C. Appeals

"[1] A student may appeal the accuracy of the report to the Suicide Prevention Team. In some instances, in order for the appeal to go forward, a student will be required to sign a release of information authorizing the members of the Suicide Prevention Team to contact and interview witnesses to the incident.

"[2] The policy of four sessions of professional assessment is applied uniformly to all students who cross the threshold described above. The requirement of four professional assessments is not subject to appeal.

"[3] If a student disagrees with other aspects of the program, such as whether the events in question cross the threshold of what constitutes a suicide threat or attempt or whether the professional he or she has retained meets the requirements of the program, he or she can appeal the Suicide Prevention Team's decision to the Dean of Students or designee. The Dean of Students decision is final."

[The abridged text of a related University of Illinois policy* memorandum]

"Date: September 24, 2002

From: Paul Joffe, Chair, Psychological Emergency Service

Re: Standard of response following a non-life threatening** suicidal incident in Housing Division and Certified Housing

"In the event that a student makes a non life-threatening suicide threat or attempt the following expectations apply:

"[1] During business hours: Within one hour, the resident director or area coordinator will contact in descending preference Paul Joffe, another member of the Suicide Prevention Team (Greg Lambeth . . ., Dave Crowley . . .), or emergency professional on duty and inform them of the incident and ask them to make a preliminary assessment and intervention plan. In the intervention plan if is determined that student needs to have an immediate face-to-face assessment, arrangements will be made for the student to be seen at either the Counseling Center or McKinley Mental Health.

"[2] Outside of business hours: Within one hour, the resident director or area coordinator will contact Crisis Team and inform them of the incident and ask them to make a preliminary assessment and intervention plan. If in the intervention plan it is determined that the student needs to participate in a face-face-assessment, it will be expected that the student will be assessed in the residence hall by the Crisis Team representative within three hours of the phone call, unless there are extenuating medical circumstances that necessitate the assessment occur in the emergency room.

"[3] If housing professionals have any concerns about an assessment or intervention occurring outside of business hours and/or want a second opinion, they are encouraged to call [me] at home . . ."

---

1. The goal of the Suicide Prevention Program is not to withdraw students and only on student has been withdrawn in the 19 year history of the program. In that case, she was readmitted three months later.

*Provided by Paul Joffe at the University of Illinois and used with permission

**In the event of a life threatening suicide incident the standard of response is 911

Appendix F

The Air Force
Suicide Prevention Program

This revised overview of the Air Force suicide program, compiled by Gary Pavela, was first published in the June 3 and June 10, 2004 issues of the ASJA Law and Policy Report.

A 2004 study in the publication *Journal Watch Psychiatry* reported that a "system-wide multi-layered" U.S. Air Force suicide prevention program begun in the mid-1990s has resulted in a significant reduction in suicide rates, and "similar or greater reductions in risks for homicide and moderate-to-severe family violence." ("A System-wide Suicide Prevention Program," February 2004, p. 15).

An overview of the Air Force program can be found at a "best practice initiative" website for the U.S. Department of Health and Human Services (HHS):

http://phs.os.dhhs.gov/ophs/BestPractice/usaf.htm

HHS reports that:

When the project began in 1995, suicide was the second leading cause of death among the 350,000 Air Force members, occurring at an annual rate of 15.8/100,000. Since then, the suicide rate declined statistically significantly over three consecutive years, and for the first six months in 1999 the annualized rate fell below 3.5/100,000. This is more than fifty percent less than the lowest rate on record prior to 1995 and an 80 percent drop from the peak rates in the mid-90s. The suicide rates increased in '00 and early '01, but have declined again since April '01 and have remained much lower than rates prior to 1995. Statistically significant declines in violent crime, family violence and deaths due to unintentional injuries have also been measured concurrently with the intervention. Air Force leaders have emphasized community-wide involvement in every aspect of the project. The providers of community-based human services have made significant progress in coordinating their resources for the purpose of building stronger individuals and more resilient communities ... The suicide rates in the United States also declined in the second half of the decade of the 1990s. This decline, however is extremely small compared to that measured in the Air Force ...

The Air Force has published a 54 page report about its suicide prevention program, available at: http://www.e-publishing.af.mil/ pubfiles/af/44/afpam44-160/afpam44-160.pdf

Excerpts from the report follow, in added question and answer format:

[What prompted development of the program?]

"In the spring of 1996, the Air Force's most senior leaders sensed that the details of far too many suicides were crossing their desks in daily reports of major events. In May of that year, the suicide of Admiral Jeremy Boorda, the top-ranking officer in the US Navy, caused them to take an even closer look. It was time to take more aggressive action against the problem of suicide among Air Force members."

[What initial steps were taken?]

"General Thomas Moorman, then the Air Force Vice Chief of Staff, commissioned the Air Force Suicide Prevention Integrated Product Team (IPT), under the leadership of Lieutenant General Charles "Chip" Roadman II. This IPT was to develop a comprehensive plan to respond to the problem. Consonant with the team leader's vision, Air Force suicide would not receive merely a medical response, but rather an Air Force response.

"To do that, representatives from the entire Air Force community had to be fully invested in the process and the result. Many Air Force agencies and individuals—Military and Civilian Personnel, the Chaplains, Safety, Staff Judge Advocate, Commanders, First Sergeants, Child and Youth Programs, Family Support, Family Advocacy, Law Enforcement, Office of Special Investigations, Epidemiology, Mental Health, and Preventive Medicine—participated. From outside the Air Force, the Centers for Disease Control and Prevention (CDC), the Armed Forces Institute of Pathology, and the Walter Reed Army Institute of Research also helped. Altogether, about 75 individuals spent June and July of 1996 assembling all that was known about Air Force suicide victims. From this initial evaluation, a plan emerged, based on expert opinion and the best available scientific knowledge. The goal was to build a prevention program that would, through its implementation, save lives."

[What data did the team gather?]

"The team established several epidemiological baselines:
• In the first half of the 1990s, suicide had been the second leading killer of airmen, responsible for 24 percent of all deaths."

• The rate of suicide had risen significantly for enlisted males, both African-American and Caucasian, in the years preceding 1996, though still about 40 percent less than the age-, sex-, and race-matched US population.

• Fewer than one third of the suicide victims had accessed Air Force mental health services before their deaths.

• From 1990 to 1995, 25 percent of suicide victims had legal problems, frequently with the military justice system. A mental health specialist had evaluated fewer than one in five.

• Of the entire constellation of risk factors, problems with relationships, the law, and finances played a part in an overwhelming majority of suicides."

[What were some of the team's initial conclusions?]

"After numerous briefings on stand-alone databases, suicide theories, and single-faceted solutions, three themes resonated with team members:

• Airmen feared losing their jobs and avoided seeking professional help because of the stigma associated with mental health problems and their treatment.

• Many airmen perceived that commanders and supervisors routinely viewed mental health records, which reinforced the barriers due to stigma.

• The Air Force was losing one of its defining qualities, a supportive interconnectedness that was best described by an old, though oft-repeated, slogan: 'The Air Force takes care of its own.'"

[Did the team find any factors that tended to protect individuals against suicide?]

"'[P]rotective' factors [fell] into three categories:

• Social support and interconnectedness;

• Individual coping skills;

• Cultural norms that promote and protect responsible help-seeking behavior."

[What principles or assumptions guided the team's work?]

"During six weeks of briefings, discussions, e-mails, and multiple drafts and redrafts, certain assumptions emerged that would underlie the remainder of the team's work:

• Many, if not most, suicides are preventable.

• Although there were no proven suicide-prevention methods, consensus recommendations from the CDC and World Health Organization were most promising.

- Suicide is not a medical problem, but a problem of the entire Air Force community.

- Suicide is the "tip of the iceberg" of psychosocial problems in the Air Force. A responsible suicide prevention program must address the entire iceberg of afflictions to individuals, families, and their communities.

- A community-based approach to reducing suicide would require committed partnerships by many different professional and social service providers.

- Only the Air Force Chief of Staff and the four-star generals could lead the way for the requisite cultural transformations that would:

    • Strengthen lifesaving social support to all Air Force members, especially those impersonal crisis, and

    • Encourage and protect those who responsibly seek mental health treatment."

[What role did Air Force leadership play?]

"Developing an effective suicide-prevention program that will reach over 370,000 airmen stationed around the globe presents significant challenges for training and program maintenance. Another barrier to an effective program is the constantly changing Air Force population, with over 30,000 new airmen entering service every year ... One way in which the Air Force Suicide Prevention Integrated Product Team (IPT) sought to keep the prevention program current and on everyone's mind was to make it a commander's program by obtaining leadership support. The Air Force is structured hierarchically. The Chief of Staff of the Air Force (CSAF) is the senior ranking officer. A primary method for transferring important information from the CSAF to the installations is through the message system. This system disseminates information rapidly throughout the Air Force. The IPT saw it as an ideal method for distributing information about suicide prevention ... The messages released by the CSAF not only show top-level support for suicide prevention, but also provide education and guidance to Air Force leaders. Messages are released every three to six months. They generally encourage commanders to:

- Actively support suicide prevention.

- Promote protective factors.

- Identify risk factors.

- Recognize suicide prevention as a community effort.

- Encourage airmen not to fear seeking help.

- Provide progress reports and information."

[What were some of the messages sent?]

"The following excerpt from a message emphasizes social support, which is a powerful protective factor:

... Please go the extra mile to foster a sense of belonging. Make sure your people feel they are a member of the team at unit functions and other small gatherings. It has been repeatedly demonstrated that social connections save lives Let's ensure we take care of our own our Air Force family ...

[signed] General Michael E. Ryan
Air Force Chief of Staff (1997-Present)

• "In addition, commanders want to be vigilant for risk factors that could increase the likelihood of a suicide or an attempt. The following is an example from a message that attempts to increase awareness of suicide risk factors:

... Since relationship problems are a factor in over half of our suicides, be vigilant for risk signs and respond with help to fellow airmen having problems ...

[signed] General Michael E. Ryan
Air Force Chief of Staff

• "Making suicide prevention a community effort is a central feature of the prevention program. The goal is to heighten awareness of suicide and to create a culture that encourages everyone to take some responsibility for this effort:

... We are not just another big corporation we are the United States Air Force, and we "take care of our own"

[signed] General Thomas Moorman
Air Force Vice Chief of Staff (1994-1997)

• "A major goal of the prevention program is to reduce the barriers to seeking help. Therefore, a number of messages encouraged commanders to communicate to their troops that it is appropriate to seek help, even mental health services:

... Communicate in your words and actions that it is not only acceptable, but a sign of strength, to recognize life problems and get professional help to deal with them constructively. This help may come from chaplains, mental health providers, family support centers, or other providers on-base or off-base. We must support and protect to the full extent possible those courageous people who seek help early, before the crisis develops a ...

[signed] General Michael E. Ryan
Air Force Chief of Staff

• "Using the message system provides a way of keeping commanders informed about the progress of the suicide prevention program:

> ... Suicides among Air Force members have fallen 37 percent, to
> the lowest rate since 1989. Since many of the risk factors involved
> are slow to change (e.g., substance abuse, mental health problems,
> failures in relationships, etc.), we can assume the decline is due pri-
> marily to strengthening protective factors: social support, effective
> personal skills for handling difficult situations, and policies and cul-
> tural norms that encourage and protect those who seek help ...

> [signed] General Michael E. Ryan
> Air Force Chief of Staff

• "Finally, messages are used to maintain a focus on suicide prevention. Sustaining the program is a major concern as it enters its fourth
year. The IPT sees messages as one way of trying to keep suicide prevention a central part of commanders' activities:

> ... we have experienced dramatic reductions in the number of Air
> Force suicides. Our efforts are working. Suicide however, continues
> to pose a threat to the health and well-being of our community and
> we cannot afford to relax our efforts ...

> [signed] General Michael E. Ryan
> Air Force Chief of Staff"

[What conclusions were reached about how suicide should be viewed?]

"In reviewing those factors that contributed to suicides, as well
as those that seemed to protect against it, it became very clear that
suicide was most effectively viewed as a command problem, rather
than a mental health problem. One statistic made this point: fewer
than one-third of Air Force suicide victims had been seen in a mental
health clinic within the last month of their lives. However, they had
all been seen at work typically as recently as the last workday before
their deaths.

"Still, it was not fair or correct simply to point fingers at commanders, first sergeants, or supervisors, and allege that they were somehow not doing their jobs. It was absolutely true that many believed
they were not adequately prepared to intervene effectively with a suicidal individual. Education for commanders, first sergeants, and supervisors, seemed to be an appropriate initiative, even though many
of them were routinely and successfully managing difficult situations
with seriously distressed individuals."

[What additional data was gathered?]

"We know from Air Force Office of Special Investigation (AFOSI)
studies that, from 1983 to 1993, the Air Force averaged one suicide

every five days. We also know, from the AFOSI studies, these facts about the suicide victims:

- 47 percent communicated their intention to kill themselves
- 53 percent gave clear indications of depression at the time of their death
- 76 percent had serious problems in their intimate relationships
- 32 percent had substance abuse problems
- 23 percent had financial problems
- 16 percent had legal problems
- 43 percent had work-related problems
- 60 percent had multiple problems."

What educational initiatives were undertaken?

"The Air Force Suicide Prevention Integrated Product Team (IPT) developed two educational initiatives to fill any real or imagined gaps in knowledge regarding suicide and helping individuals who were suicidal:

- "General community training (see Chapter V of this report) Annual community training with a limited set of basic learning objectives on identifying individuals in distress and guidelines for taking appropriate action.

- "Professional military education (PME) More extensive periodic training for Air Force members, in greater depth and specifically oriented to an individual's rank and level of responsibility. Most individuals who stay in the Air Force beyond their initial obligation attend rank-appropriate PME. Therefore, the IPT determined that PME curricula should be reviewed and, where appropriate, changes and/or additions should be proposed that address suicide prevention.

"Perhaps the most difficult aspect of the educational initiatives has been getting additional information included in PME curricula, which are always very full. There are many and diverse demands to include instructional blocks on specific areas of interest. A typical response from a PME course director is, "Show me what I should drop to make room for your block." Support for the suicide risk-reduction initiatives came from the highest levels of authority on the Air Staff, which helped clear the way."

How were personnel encouraged to seek help?

"The IPT [Integrated Product Team] sent a briefing to all Air Force installations and mental health facilities, with a cover letter from the Chief of Staff of the Air Force directing that every commander in the

Air Force receive the briefing and put its message into practice. Commanders were to encourage early self-referral to mental health, and unequivocally communicate to subordinates that 'It's okay to get help.' This message was considered important enough to convene all Air Force commanders and first sergeants for the sole purpose of hearing the briefing.

"The briefing repeatedly underscores that effective leaders help their people seek care early, and are instrumental in removing barriers and stigma associated with needing care. An individual life-enhancement, mission-performance opportunity is captured by an early referral. The briefing states that every member of the Air Force community (commanders, first sergeants, supervisors, friends, and family) participate in recognizing and getting help for those who are struggling to cope with difficult life events. Commanders and supervisors, in particular, are in a powerful position to dispel concerns about seeking help. They can also facilitate obtaining such help. Commanders are given data to counteract the perception that seeking mental health care is a career-ending move. There is evidence to suggest that members who refer themselves are unlikely to experience a negative career impact."

[What role was given to prevention?]

"Historically, prevention services were not officially accounted for on existing manpower standards, and so any agency providing these services was in danger of losing personnel. This 'prevention penalty' discouraged the delivery of community preventive services. For instance, in calendar year 1997, the ratio of prevention services to all mental health services was about 0.7 percent, the equivalent of only 8 full-time positions providing prevention services for the entire Air Force. Getting mental health personnel into the community and performing a prevention role serves many functions. Only about one-third of those who committed suicide had received mental health care or intervention. Many view seeking such help in the military environment as a sign of weakness, at best, and a career killer, at worst.

"The IPT considered that putting mental health personnel into the community to serve in prevention/non-clinical roles was a first step to removing the stigma associated with seeking traditional mental health care. Second, it allows mental health professionals earlier access to those who are suffering. Third, mental health personnel provide these preventive/educational encounters without record keeping. The hope was that the lack of a written record would encourage an atmosphere where information could be exchanged more freely ...

"Time spent in prevention activities tripled in 1998 and remained steady through 1999. However, we have not reached the goal of dedicating five percent of all mental health activities to prevention. The rate of activity leveled off at two percent, or the equivalent of 26 FTEs Air Force-wide. Air Force consultants for psychiatry, psychology, and social work monitor this data and establish priorities for prevention activities."

[What education and training was provided?]

"[T]he required training included four different intervention levels.

"Level One Individual

Level One was buddy care. This involved basic awareness training, with emphasis on stress and suicide risk factors. This training was conducted annually and at all levels of professional military education. The training encouraged the early identification and referral of potentially at-risk individuals to supervisors in Level Two.

"Level Two Unit Gatekeepers

Level Two involved identifying at-risk personnel (triage) and mentoring. This training equipped squadron supervisors with the tools necessary to act as a gateway to help those in need. Mentoring for supervisors would assist this effort and was a natural complement to the 'buddy care' concept encouraged in Level One. Referrals were to be made to community resources within Level Three, such as the Family Support Center or chaplains, or directly to Level Four (medical professionals) in emergencies.

"Level Three Community Gatekeepers

Level Three involved those in the helping professions at each base. A base helping professions team (Family Support Center, Chaplain, Mental Health, Family Advocacy, Child and Youth Services, and Health and Wellness Center) was to be established to network and coordinate service delivery to those in need.

"Level Four Medical Professionals

Level Four involved direct care. All medical providers were trained in identifying, referring, and treating persons at risk ...

"By 1999, over 90 percent of all active duty and civilian personnel had received some form of suicide prevention training."

[What were key components of the training?]

"Air Force Instruction (AFI) 44-154, Suicide Prevention Education and Community Training, adapts elements from the Air Education and Training Command (AETC) LINK suicide prevention program. It requires annual training in basic suicide risk factors, intervention skills, and referral procedures for people potentially at risk. AETC designed the LINK program as a preventive 'web' of individuals, supervisors, first sergeants, commanders, the community, and medical professionals to create circles of concern. Most suicidal individuals want to live, but many are unable to see alternatives to their problems. They often view their situations as hopeless. The LINK program "links" people to helping resources and alternatives.

"The goal of the LINK program is to improve the early identification and referral of potentially at-risk personnel to prevent the loss of life from suicide, other self-defeating behavior, or behavior that may place others at risk. This program attempts to reach this goal by:

• Decreasing the stigma associated with seeking help;

• Promoting early identification and referral of individuals at risk by those who know them best: their friends and co-workers;

• Encouraging supervisors to act as gateways to helping resources.

"'LINK' describes actions each person can take to help prevent suicides, and is the theme of the program:

Look for possible concerns.

Inquire about concerns.

Note level of risk.

Know referral resources and strategies."

[Was there a connection between disciplinary action and suicide?]

"In mid-1996, over 30 percent of active duty suicide victims had legal problems and most were under some type of investigation. At that time, no policy existed to ensure individuals under investigation were being assessed for suicide potential, or were receiving adequate social and psychological support while undergoing investigation. In August 1996, the IPT began drafting a policy to assist those individuals under investigation with their emotional and psychological needs. A combined effort over the next several months involving the personnel, legal, security forces, medical, and inspector general communities led to agreement, in November 1996, on the following policy tenets:

• Agencies and unit leaders share responsibility for the safety and well being of individuals who are under investigation and may be experiencing significant stress as a result of the investigation.

• All Air Force investigators (e.g., Inspector General, Equal Opportunity and Treatment, Equal Employment Opportunity, Security Forces, or Office of Special Investigations) will notify/refer an individual's first sergeant, commander, or supervisor, through person-to-person, documented contact, that the individual was interviewed and notified that they were under investigation.

• Individuals appearing emotionally distraught or stunned will be released only to their first sergeant, commander, supervisor, or designee, and are not allowed to depart from an interview or interrogation alone.

• Ensure that those agencies that do not have the legal right to detain an individual make reasonable efforts to 'hand off' an individual to a representative from their unit. If that is not possible, they must make notification as soon as possible.

• Unit leaders will take individuals experiencing stress that puts them at risk for suicide to a helping agency for professional care and services. This policy was not designed to circumvent any legal rights of the individual (e.g., the right to an attorney, the right against self-incrimination), or to create any rights not required by law. The Air Force Chief of Staff signed a policy letter incorporating those tenets, to be effective immediately, on 4 December 1996. This policy appears to have been effective. To date, no life has been lost because involved agencies did not support it. The policy has been adopted as a requirement in Department of Defense Directive 6490.1, Mental Health Evaluations of Military Members (October 1997), and Department of Defense Instruction 6490.4, Mental Health Evaluations of Military Members (October 1997), that address the issues of mental health evaluations and the concept of imminent dangerousness."

[Is suicide associated with exposure to trauma, including other suicides?]

"Experiences with combat veterans throughout the history of war have repeatedly indicated that feelings repressed become feelings expressed, and not always in the best way. Following the Vietnam war, work with veterans from that era led to an improved understanding that exposure to trauma can have long-term effects on an individual's daily functioning. This knowledge resulted in identifying a pattern of behavior now referred to as post-traumatic stress disorder (PTSD).

"Recognizing the long-term effects of PTSD is helping prevent people who are exposed to trauma from developing PTSD. Research and literature over the past 20 years have contributed to current PTSD prevention approaches. Investigators got their first exposure to a particular approach to PTSD prevention while watching the extensive coverage of the bombing of the Murrah Federal Building in Oklahoma City, in 1995. This approach is referred to as Critical Incident Stress Management (CISM).

"The Air Force Suicide Prevention Integrated Product Team (IPT) surveyed Air Force major commands to assess established procedures for responding to trauma. The survey results revealed a wide range in the levels and types of responses, and an absence of specific Air

Force guidance. Understanding the potential impact of a completed suicide on survivors, the IPT determined that an integral part of any comprehensive approach to suicide prevention would include CISM.

"The IPT helped develop Air Force Instruction (AFI) 44-153, Critical Incident Stress Management, to guide the Air Force in responding to traumatic events, including completed suicides. The AFI addresses the full spectrum of who, what, when, where, and how to respond. For the first time, the Air Force required trained, multi-disciplinary teams at each installation to respond to local traumatic events. Rather than using only mental health personnel, the AFI established multi-disciplinary teams composed of mental health providers, medical providers, and chaplains, along with senior non-commissioned officers in non-medical positions. The benefits of multi-disciplinary Critical Incident Stress Teams (CIST) include:

• Reducing the impression, and potential stigma, that CISM is only for those who need to see a mental health provider.

• Broadening the skills, perspectives, and expertise delivered to participants.

• Reducing the impact on any one unit in responding to a traumatic event. The success of the CISM initiative depends on an understanding by commanders, supervisors, and those supervised that responding to a traumatic event is difficult. The goal of CISM is to help survivors identify, through a group experience, the normalcy of their various individual responses. CISM helps replace the internal question of "What's wrong with me," and lessens the impact on feelings of those who might think "I'm the only one feeling this way."

"The CISM AFI establishes a CIST responsibility for training peer-support volunteers at each facility. This trained cadre of volunteers can better identify with a particular unit's perspective in helping it respond to a traumatic event.

"The CISM AFI also includes a prevention component, which has the goal of providing anticipatory guidance for how to deal most effectively with an anticipated traumatic event. A curriculum for pre-exposure preparation (PEP) is part of the AFI. The curriculum includes core content, facilitator guidance, and material for commanders and supervisors in understanding the purpose and goals of PEP. The PEP training is conducted primarily in two ways:

• Periodic prevention training for initial responder groups, such as security forces, firefighters, and emergency medical technicians;

• 'Just in time' training for personnel being deployed to potentially threatening environments.

"The CISM AFI was adopted in July 1997. Within the following year, all Air Force installations had established CISTs composed of members from many disciplines. These teams had responded to a wide variety of events, including completed suicides. Commanders familiar with CISM through their own participation began requesting additional sessions, to address members who worked shifts. Commanders of security forces, firefighters, and emergency medical personnel have continued to request periodic PEP training for their personnel, to enhance the state of force readiness."

[What else has been learned about suicide risk factors?]

"[I]t was soon apparent that suicide was just the tip of the iceberg. Initial epidemiological analysis demonstrated that the issues and risk factors that underlie suicide have multiple outcomes; suicide is rare. In fact, these risk factors more often underlie other human problems on which we focus many of our other support programs.

"These common risk factors include problems with;

- Relationships,
- Finances,
- Job performance,
- Legal system,
- Substance abuse and mental health, especially depression."

[How is the delivery of services coordinated?]

"The Integrated Delivery System (IDS) is one of the major programmatic recommendations proposed by the Air Force Suicide Prevention Integrated Product Team (IPT). The IPT's specific charter was to examine completed suicides in the Air Force as a community and as a leadership concern ...

"Many Air Force agencies provide broad-based prevention services that focus on these risk factors, reduce stress, and improve the coping skills and general well being of individuals and families. While each agency has a unique mission, they all share a common prevention mission, in which there may be overlaps, duplication, or gaps. Given such a diversity of agencies and programs, customers found it difficult to access and navigate the system. One agency's marketing efforts often inadvertently created a sense of competition with another, which confused the customer.

"Many bases attempted ad hoc coordination, to increase the availability of programs and services. However, these attempts were not consistent Air Force-wide in addressing wasteful duplications or service gaps. Without a coordinated system, customers (both commanders and members) often did not get the service they desired or needed. The intent of the IDS is to establish a seamless system of services, made up of collaborative partnerships and coordinated human-service preventive activities for individuals and families. This system streamlines access and establishes new links among participating helping agencies. The six primary IDS agencies that have significant prevention-based resources dedicated to these issues are;

- Chaplains,
- Child and youth programs,
- Family Advocacy,
- Family Support,
- Health promotion/Health and Wellness Centers,
- Mental health clinics.

"The IDS has four primary functions;
- Centralized information and referral (I and R),
- Assessment of unit and community behavioral risk factors,
- Delivery of prevention services that are targeted to a wide range of individuals and groups within Air Force communities (leaders, active duty members and their families, civilian employees, and Reserve component members and their families),
- Collaborative marketing of IDS I and R and prevention services.

"The IDS exists as a virtual matrixed function, rather than a traditional agency. As such, it is defined by its activity rather than its location. IDS offers its services at work sites, schools, and community facilities, as well as at any of the member agency facilities. The IDS is chartered as a standing subcommittee of the installation Community Action Information Board (CAIB). (The CAIB is a cross-functional committee made up of community agencies and chaired by a senior military officer on the installation, usually the Wing Commander or the Vice Commander.) Core membership of the IDS includes, but is not limited to, leadership representatives from each of the six primary agencies. Since prevention is a community-wide concern, any program or agency not specifically mentioned is welcome to participate in collaborating, coordinating, and marketing these efforts.

"The installation commander annually appoints a representative from one of the primary agencies to act as the IDS coordinator in his or her behalf. In making this appointment, the installation commander ensures the full cooperation of each agency contributing services to the IDS function. As the installation commander's representative, the coordinator is responsible for facilitating and directing collaborative efforts within the IDS team, and between the IDS team and the community. The coordinator reports to the installation commander at least quarterly on the progress of the IDS. Initial policy guidance to installations in support of this significant effort was broad, rather than prescriptive. It provided for maximum flexibility in meeting local needs, based on local requirements and resources. Rather than specifying a 'one-size-fits-all' model for the IDS, the bottom-line requirements are twofold:

• Create a collaborative, integrated, and customer-focused prevention delivery system;

• Achieve meaningful and measurable outcomes for the community.

"One year following their initial development, IDS teams were operational on all Air Force installations. Many innovative best practices were identified. However, the need was apparent for a formal management structure, outside the Suicide Prevention IPT, to provide oversight and ongoing guidance for IDS implementation across the Air Force. The establishment of the Air Force CAIB (Air Force Instruction 90-500, Community Action Information Boards), chaired by the assistant vice chief of staff, provided an ideal response to this gap. (Note: The assistant vice chief of staff is the third highest position in the United States Air Force.) The Air Force CAIB elevates IDS issues from functional concerns to Air Force issues, and provides senior Air Force leadership visibility for these important quality-of life issues."

[What major conclusions have been reached about the program?]
"Suicide rates have fallen significantly since the inception of the Air Force Suicide Prevention Program. In addition, we have taken a number of positive steps toward making this an effective program:

• Actively involving leadership;

• Breaking down traditional 'stove pipes' among helping services;

• Striving to remove the stigma of seeking help;

• Creating the first privileged communication for suicidal personnel who are under criminal investigation;

• Encouraging the responsibility of all Air Force members to care for one another 'buddy care.'

"Although we can temporally relate the drop in suicides to the beginning of the prevention program, we have not established a definitive causal link. This means that it is difficult to prove that the suicide prevention program is the real, or only, reason for the reduction of suicides. When we began to design the program, we found no proven suicide-prevention methods. Therefore, we used consensus recommendations from the Centers for Disease Control and Prevention and other expert consultants in the field of suicidology to identify the basic components of this community-based approach.

"Since no causal link has been established, future program initiatives strive to maximize the recommendations of the Air Force Suicide Prevention Integrated Product Team and other consultants. These first few years were very encouraging and, in 1999, the Air Force had one of the lowest rates of suicide in its history. However, even with these impressive results, we have work to do in 1999, a historically low suicide rate still meant over 20 Air Force members died from self-inflicted injuries.

"The Air Force Suicide Prevention Integrated Product Team continues to meet regularly to identify critical areas for program improvement. As the prevention program enters its fourth year, trying to sustain a global program and high quality interventions is challenging. The goal is to maintain the highest quality possible and to keep the program focused on those factors we believe are crucial to its success:

• Leadership involvement;

• Education at all levels;

• Re-engineering helping services;

• Unit behavioral assessment;

• Surveillance."

Appendix G

A Reflection on the Columbine Report

Many school shootings are also suicides or attempted suicides. Understanding the rage and alienation of school shooters may provide insight into the disoriented thinking that often accompanies other kinds of suicidal behavior. This essay originally appeared in two issues of Synfax Weekly Report *(01.20 and 01.21, pp. 2008-2012) published in 2001.*

For many young adults the tragedy at Columbine was a searing moment in their lives. College administrators, however, are sometimes inclined to see the Columbine shootings as a "high school issue," and relegate it to secondary importance. They shouldn't. The report by the State of *Colorado Columbine Review Commission* ("Commission") contains insights that will be valuable to anyone interested in the inner lives of adolescents and young adults, and how best to respond when those lives go awry, and violence is threatened, or has occurred.

Three pertinent excerpts from the Commission's report follow (in question and answer format).

[Is the homicidal rage evident in school shootings often associated with suicide? If so, what can be done about the problem of youth suicide?]
"The subject of suicide is deeply entangled at Columbine. Obviously the attack at Columbine High School can be viewed from one perspective as a double suicide by two deeply troubled young men. But the possibility of other suicides also has become ... a direct by-product of the Columbine attack ... [T]he possibility that Columbine will harvest future victims is a legitimate matter of concern ... In this dimension the impact of the Columbine attack proved national in scope. For young persons attending school at the time, Columbine became, in the words of one college admissions director, 'a defining moment for that generation ...'

"Today, many of the myths surrounding suicide have been shown to be exactly that: myths. For example, the view that no one should dare to discuss suicide with a troubled person has been found to have no basis in fact. In actuality, the teenage years are very difficult for many young people, and many teenagers have thought about suicide at one time or another. Experts believe that troubled persons who are asked about suicide will often feel relief at being asked the question, for that frequently opens doors allowing troubled persons to discuss their problems with greater freedom ...

"Much has been learned about suicide and its warning signs; faculty and staff at our schools need to be conversant with the common warning signs for suicide and the appropriate responses and nonresponses to them when observed."

[Do school shooters often signal their plans?]

"In the wake of the events at Columbine High School, and other instances of school violence, many experts, as well as federal agencies including the Secret Service and the FBI, have studied the phenomenon in an effort to understand it. Expert witnesses before the Commission emphasized that instances of school violence do not occur because students 'suddenly snapped,' due to a particular incident on a particular day. Instead, school shooters usually give very clear advance indications of their violent intentions, so that school officials and law enforcement agencies are in fact able to prevent violence whenever (1) they have information about such threats; (2) they are able to draw together information about dangerous students from a variety of sources; (3) the authorities understand how to evaluate the threats. Experts who study school violence refer to this spectrum of direct and indirect communications by perpetrators in advance of an event as 'leakage.'"

[What can be done to challenge the student "code of silence?"]

"Students may well not understand that even jokes about violence or indirect threats of violence may be significant. Schools have begun to work to change this code of silence by talking to students about the limits of loyalty to friends ... One way to encourage students to report their concerns about potential violence, without their having to worry about repercussions, is to put in place a mechanism through which students may report their concerns or worries anonymously."

COMMENTARY
by Gary Pavela

The Columbine Commission report contained many practical insights for educators, beyond the excerpts cited above. What the Commission did not do was offer a consistent interpretation of the values and beliefs that may have motivated Columbine killers Dylan Klebold and Eric Harris. We think such an interpretation is possible, and that educators who consider it will be better able to offer an antidote to what is essentially a *philosophical* disorder: The dogmatic misapplication of Darwinian theory to all aspects of life.

Evidence of suicidal rage ...

The Commission report highlights the suicidal rage displayed by Klebold and Harris—a rage that was telegraphed to the world on Harris' AOL website:

> I'm coming for EVERYONE soon and I WILL be armed to the f___ing teeth and I WILL shoot to kill. God, I can't wait until I kill you people. Feel no remorse, no sense of shame, I don't care if I live or die in the shoot-out. All I want to do is to kill and injure as many of you ... as I can ...

The Commission report indicated that both of the Columbine shooters displayed signs of depression. Harris was taking antidepressant medication, and had a significant level of the medication in his system when he committed suicide. The killers' depression may have been exacerbated by a sense of social isolation from most of their peers.

And the philosophical perspective that fanned it.

Comparatively few people with clinical depression attempt to harm themselves or others. Likewise, people who feel socially isolated display many different coping strategies, including efforts to develop deeper friendships with fellow "outcasts." Why did Klebold and Harris resort to a massacre?

The complexity of Klebold's and Harris' motivation was highlighted by their apparent selection of random victims (virtually everyone was a target) and by a deliberate effort to fan their own feelings of anger and alienation. Writers for *Time Magazine* reviewed five secret videotapes the killers recorded before the shootings (*Special Report: The Columbine Tapes*), and reported that:

> It is clear listening to them that Harris and Klebold were not just having trouble with what their counselors called "anger management." They fed the anger, fueled it, so the fury could take hold, because they knew they would need it to do what they had set out to do. "More rage. More rage," Harris says. "Keep building it on," he says, motioning with his hands for emphasis.

The Columbine Commission described Harris and Klebold as "above average, if not gifted, students." Is it possible they had thought about a philosophical perspective that could be used to justify and channel their feelings? The answer is yes, and it can be found in footnote 51 of the Commission report:

> They noted that they had evolved above "you humans." The two seemed fascinated with the notion of natural selection: "what-

ever happened to natural selection?," Klebold asked on the tapes as he spoke of his hatred of the human race. On his web page Harris called natural selection "... the best thing that has ever happened to the Earth. Getting rid of all the stupid and weak organisms ..." Harris also inscribed in a female friend's 1998 yearbook that "natural selection needs a boost, like me with a shotgun." At the time of his death, Harris was wearing a T-shirt with the words "Natural Selection" printed across the front.

Every aspect of Klebold's and Harris' last day seems to have been carefully choreographed. They had many messages to send, at many levels. What's remarkable is how little attention has been paid to the words "Natural Selection" displayed across Harris' chest.

Echoes of a prior killing

Americans are not a philosophical people, attuned to philosophical perspectives. So it would be easy to read about the Columbine shootings and miss a connection with another famous case involving two bright young murderers: The 1924 killing of fourteen-year-old Bobby Franks by Nathan Leopold and Richard Loeb (one a student at the University of Chicago; the other a precocious UC graduate, planning to go to Harvard Law School). Leopold and Loeb apparently killed Franks as an intellectual challenge, to alleviate boredom and commit "the perfect crime."

Clarence Darrow represented Leopold and Loeb, and helped them escape the death penalty. He made good use of psychiatric testimony, even if it seemed superficially unfavorable to his clients. One doctor testified that:

All of [Loeb's] life, from the beginning of his antisocial activities, has been in the direction of his own self-destruction. He himself has definitely and seriously considered suicide ...

Another doctor said

I was amazed at the absolute absence of any signs of normal feelings [in Loeb], such as one would expect under the circumstances. He showed no remorse, no regret, no compassion for the people involved in this situation ...

Darrow's summary argument is cited in law schools to this day. One section of that argument focused on Leopold's philosophical perspectives, and how they suited Loeb's lack of conscience:

Babe [Leopold] is ... a boy of remarkable mind—away beyond his years. He is a sort of freak in this direction, as in others; a boy without emotions, a boy obsessed of philosophy ... He went through school quickly; he went to college young; he could learn faster than almost everybody else. His emotional life was lacking ...

Babe took to philosophy ... He became enamored of the philosophy of Nietzsche ... Nietzsche believed that some time the superman would be born, that evolution was working toward the superman. He wrote one book, "Beyond Good and Evil," which was a criticism of all moral codes as the world understands them; a treatise holding that the intelligent man is beyond good and evil; that the laws for good and the laws for evil do not apply to those who approach the superman.

Babe was obsessed of it, and here are some of the things which Nietzsche taught: Become hard. To be obsessed by moral consideration presupposes a very low grade of intellect. We should substitute for morality the will to our own end, and consequently to the means to accomplish that. Nietzsche held a contemptuous, scornful attitude to all those things which the young are taught as important in life; a fixing of new values which are not the values by which any normal child has ever yet been reared—a philosophical dream, containing more or less truth, that was not meant by anyone to be applied to life ...

It was not a casual bit of philosophy with [Leopold]; it was his life. He believed in a superman. He and Dickie Loeb were the supermen. There might have been others, but they were two, and two chums. The ordinary commands of society were not for him. Many of us read this philosophy but know that it has no actual application to life; but not he. It became a part of his being. It was his philosophy. He lived it and practiced it; he thought it applied to him, and he could not have believed it excepting that it either caused a diseased mind or was the result of diseased mind.

Taking philosophy seriously

Two case studies of homicide and youthful alienation seventy-five years apart don't make a definitive argument. But there is a view expressed by psychologist Stanton Samenow (author of *Inside the Criminal Mind*, New York Times Books, 1984) and Psychiatrist Willard Gaylin (author of *The Killing of Bonnie Garland*, Simon and Schuster, 1982) that criminal acts often reflect what Samenow calls "the chessboard view of life"—a sense that one has risen above ordinary considerations of good and evil, and that victims are sheep. This is not a "mental disorder": *it is a philosophical assumption about how the world works.* Educators who fail to see that fact will leave students unprepared to participate in serious discussions about the possibility of better alternatives.

A fundamental question needs to be explored. Are human beings passive actors on the evolutionary stage, or do we see and represent a moral dimension perhaps contributing to moral progress? The subject, at a minimum, is worthy of serious consideration, as suggested in a letter written by Charles Darwin to a colleague at Harvard University (cited by the late Stephen J. Gould in his 1999 book *Rock of Ages: Science and Religion in the Fullness of Life*, Ballantine, pp. 35-35):

I own that I cannot see as plainly as others do, and as I should wish to do, evidence of design and beneficence on all sides of us.

There seems to me too much misery in the world ... On the other hand, I cannot somehow be contented to view this wonderful universe and especially the nature of man, and to conclude that everything is the result of brute force ... I feel most deeply that the whole subject is too profound for the human intellect. A dog might as well speculate on the mind of Newton.

Darwin's humility about ultimate knowledge (combined with a receptivity to hints of beauty and harmony in the universe) reflects one of the best qualities of the scientific spirit. It is a quality lacking in new converts to any dogma, including social Darwinism—which can acquire a cult-like following among self-inflated adolescents. Educators have a duty to challenge that kind of narrow-mindedness, as they would any other.